RENT CONTROL
A POPULAR PARADOX

RENT CONTROL
A POPULAR PARADOX

Evidence on the Economic Effects of Rent Control

by F.A. Hayek,
Milton Friedman and George J. Stigler,
Bertrand de Jouvenel, F.W. Paish,
F.G. Pennance, E.O. Olsen,
Sven Rydenfelt,
M.A. Walker

Published by

The Fraser Institute

Canadian Shared Cataloguing in Publication Data
Main entry under title:
Rent control, a popular paradox
ISBN 0-88975-000-9 pa. (trade)
ISBN 0-88975-007-6 pa. (mass market)
1. Housing—Canada. 2. Rent control.
I. Hayek, Friedrich August von, 1899-
II. Friedman, Milton, 1912- III.
Fraser Institute.
HD7305.A3R45 301.5'4'0971

First published 1975 by the Fraser Institute.
ISBN 0-88975-000-9 (Trade paperback edition)
First printing . . . . . . October, 1975
Second printing . . . . November, 1975
Third printing . . . . . January, 1976
ISBN 0-88975-007-6 (Mass market paperback edition)
First printing . . . . . . August, 1976

Printed in Canada.

Contents

PART III — WHAT IS THE SOLUTION?

Preface

A common ground

Every well-intentioned person who concerns himself with the economic problems of housing has the same basic objective, namely to determine the best way to provide every Canadian with access to the "best possible standard of housing". A similar statement of objectives could be made about most aspects of Canadian life — "best possible health care", "best possible standard of nutrition", "best possible transportation system" etc. It is obvious that with limited resources, the notion of "best possible" must be taken to mean "best possible given the need to improve other aspects of our standard of living". In approaching the problem of housing we must, therefore, recognize the limitations that the need to satisfy other objectives places on the "possible" rate of progress toward our goal.

Who decides?

Given that there are many competing uses for our limited resources, who should decide which of our standard of living objectives is pursued most vigorously? There are two basic answers to this question and a bewildering variety of answers in between that are combinations of the two basic answers. The basic answers are — 1. Each individual should decide the way in which his or her efforts are used in the attainment of his or her personal goals. — 2. The state should decide how the collective effort of individuals is applied in the attainment of a selected set of social goals.

From a purely economic point of view, the choice between these two answers should be made on the basis of which will most surely achieve the objective of maximizing the standard of living of each member of the society. Generally speaking, Canada has had a tradition of allowing economic decisions to be made on the basis of individual pursuit of individual goals. This tradition was clearly reflected in the Report of the Senate Committee on National Finance, "Growth, Employment and Price Stability".[1]

> "Our . . . guiding principle is that the Canadian economy should remain a predominantly market system . . . in which the bulk of productive and distributive activity is carried out by private enterprise units responsive to consumer demand . . ."

Intervention — when and why?

To the extent that the state intervenes in economic affairs the process of choice moves beyond the control of the individual and into the hands of the "state" which in practical terms means into the hands of the government bureaucracy. Because intervention causes a loss of individual choice, each instance of intervention must be clearly justifiable on the grounds that it improves the overall condition of every Canadian. If this principle does not guide government intervention then the net result of such intervention will invariably be a loss in individual choice with no improvement in, or even a deterioration,of the standard of living.

In an increasing number of cases, government intervention occurs because some special interest group creates pressure for "the government to do something". The decision, by government, to intervene is too often based on an assessment of the so-called "political realities"; the fact that the economic realities suggest that intervention will be disastrous gets lost in the maze of political expediency.

The role of the economist

The responsibility of the economist in matters of public policy analysis is to assess objectively the likely course of events in the absence of intervention; to determine the likely effects of intervention, and finally, if intervention is clearly justified on economic grounds, to determine the most constructive form of government intervention.

Very often the economist's attention focuses on an intervention, or series of interventions, after the fact. (This is largely because many interventions are undertaken for

[1] *Report of the Standing Senate Committee on National Finance on "Growth, Employment, and Price Stability"*, Information Canada, 1971, Page 3.

purely political reasons and hence are not scrutinized for their economic impact). This greatly complicates the task of assessing objectively the effects of the intervention. In other cases, the intervention is so pervasive or is of such long standing, that it has become institutionalized. If "institutionalization" has occurred but the intervention is clearly harmful, the economist is then confronted with the task of proposing policy action that will be regarded as "politically impossible". To the extent that the economist as policy analyst fails in this task and permits political expediency to affect his policy recommendations he fails to serve the public interest.

Rent control

Rent control is a form of government intervention that is being suggested with greater frequency in Canada as a solution to "the housing problem". Two provinces have already adopted it in some form and pressure from tenant groups is rising in other provinces. In view of this rising tide of opinion and given what must be called the "disastrous" experience of other countries with rent control, The Fraser Institute has undertaken this book of essays to provide a factual consideration of the housing problem and the solution to it that rent control is said to offer.

What is the problem?

The first part of the book endeavours to determine the nature of the housing problem. That process also provides a concise documentation of current and past housing conditions in Canada. It will come as a surprise to some to learn that current conditions were anticipated as early as 1966 and exactly foreseen and documented in 1970.

The conclusion that the available information, our analysis of the information and the analysis of others, suggests is that there is not a housing problem in the sense that there is something wrong with the rental housing market. The housing market is responding in a perfectly predictable fashion to the policies and events of the past five or six years. There is, however, and has been for some time, a poverty problem — a problem that has been exacerbated by the fact that the pressure of policies and events is beginning to force rents up.

Is rent control the solution?

The central question that is addressed in Part II is whether or not rent control is a solution to this problem — or to any "housing" problem. In assembling essays on the economic effects of rent control, we attempted to provide an objective selection of source material. Under normal circumstances this would be expected to produce a range of views on the topic at hand.

Strange as it may seem to the casual observer of the economics profession, there appears to be a unique unanimity of opinion among economists about the effects of rent control. The extent of the agreement is indicated by the remarks of the 1974 Nobel Prize winners in economics, Gunnar Myrdal and Friedrich Hayek, whose views on matters other than rent control are, ideologically speaking, quite different. Paul Samuelson, 1970 winner of the Nobel award, described their general views as follows:

> "in no sense has their work been joint. Indeed, their policy conclusions if followed literally would be at loggerheads and self-cancelling".[2]

Gunnar Myrdal, who Samuelson described as "an important architect of the Swedish Labour Party's Welfare State", had the following low opinion of rent control and those who implement it:

> "Rent control has in certain western countries constituted, maybe, the worst example of poor planning by governments lacking courage and vision".[3]

Friedrich Hayek, author of the best seller, *Road to Serfdom* and one of the most respected intellectual defenders of free choice as the basis for human conduct, in an essay in this volume, says of rent control:

> "If this account seems to boil down to a catalogue of iniquities to be laid at the door of rent control, that is

[2] Paul Samuelson, New York Times, October 10, 1974.

[3] Quoted in, "The Rise and Fall of Swedish Rent Control" in this volume.

> no mere coincidence, but inevitable . . . I doubt very much whether theoretical research into the same problems carried out by someone of a different politico-economic persuasion than myself could lead to different conclusions. Therefore, if theory brings to light nothing but unfavourable conclusions, it must indicate that though the immediate benefits of rent control, for which it was introduced in the first place, are obvious to everyone, theory is needed to uncover the unintentional consequences which intervention brings in its wake".[4]

Thus, although the reader will not find essays in this book that would lend any support to rent control as an aspect of housing policy, it can be accurately said that the essays do reflect the range of opinion of economists.

In view of the fact that rent control is not a solution and should, therefore, be abandoned, an essay on the likely consequences of immediate decontrol has been included. Of special concern in that essay is the "political realities" bogeyman that is often associated with suggestions for gradual decontrol. The finding of that essay, based on detailed information about decontrol in the United States, is that none of the feared consequences of immediate decontrol appear to occur.

An income supplement

The final section of the book develops an income supplementation formula designed to protect all Canadians from the hardship associated with the rising cost of *basic* shelter. In the process of developing the formula a critical analysis of a scheme suggested by Dennis and Fish is undertaken. The suggestion is made that their formula and others like it be avoided because they are designed to provide people with a subsidy on the basis of what they *actually do* spend on housing instead of on the basis of what they *must* spend. The formula that we suggest is tied to the cost of *basic* shelter on a regional basis and accordingly, an income supplementation program built around it would probably be self-liquidating.

Some of the essays in Part II have appeared in other

[4] "The Repercussions of Rent Restriction", reprinted in this volume.

publications and earlier versions of five of them appeared in The Institute of Economic Affairs' publication, "*Verdict on Rent Control*".[5] The paper on the effects of rent control in New York City by Professor Olsen was written specially for this volume, as were substantial portions of Professor Rydenfelt's and Professor Pennance's. Professor Pennance has also provided an introduction to the international section, while Parts I and III were prepared by The Fraser Institute.

[5] *Verdict on Rent Control*, Ed. by Arthur Seldon, Institute of Economic Affairs, London, 1972.

PART I

What Is The Problem?

What are the Facts?

M.A. WALKER

Chief Economist, The Fraser Institute

HISTORICAL PERSPECTIVE

In a study of housing for the Federal Minister of Housing, the Hon. R.K. Andras, in 1971,[1] Professor L.B. Smith set out to establish if a housing problem did indeed exist, and, if so, what the nature of the problem was. A consideration of the available information led Smith to several conclusions about housing and housing policy as they then were, and to make several forecasts about what the future held. In view of the fact that Smith's analysis and forecasts have proved remarkably accurate, we selected his work as the point of departure for our own analysis of the "housing problem".

The first section of this essay consists of a re-examination of Smith's conclusions and forecasts in the light of subsequent events. In the course of this re-examination we will be providing an historical perspective on some aspects of the current state of housing in Canada and an analysis of the current "problem".

Smith's first conclusion in 1970:

> 'To the extent that our nation is better housed than ever in terms of number and basic facilities, there is no immediate housing problem.'

Smith's second conclusion in 1970:

> 'To the extent that our construction industry has averaged approximately 200,000 dwelling starts per year for the last two years (the Economic Council of Canada's target) and can provide numerically sufficient dwellings for our population, there is no housing crisis.'

[1] *Urban Canada — Problems and Prospects;* Research Monograph 2, L.B. Smith, *Housing in Canada;* Ottawa, 1971.

Smith's fourth conclusion in 1970:

> 'To the extent that there are fewer doubled families (180,000 or 4 per cent of all families in Canada in 1966) and considerable numbers of non-family households, there is no housing problem.'[2]

More houses than households

At the time Smith wrote his report (1970) it would have been very difficult to conclude anything but that the housing market was functioning very effectively in providing Canadians (on average) with an increased standard of housing.

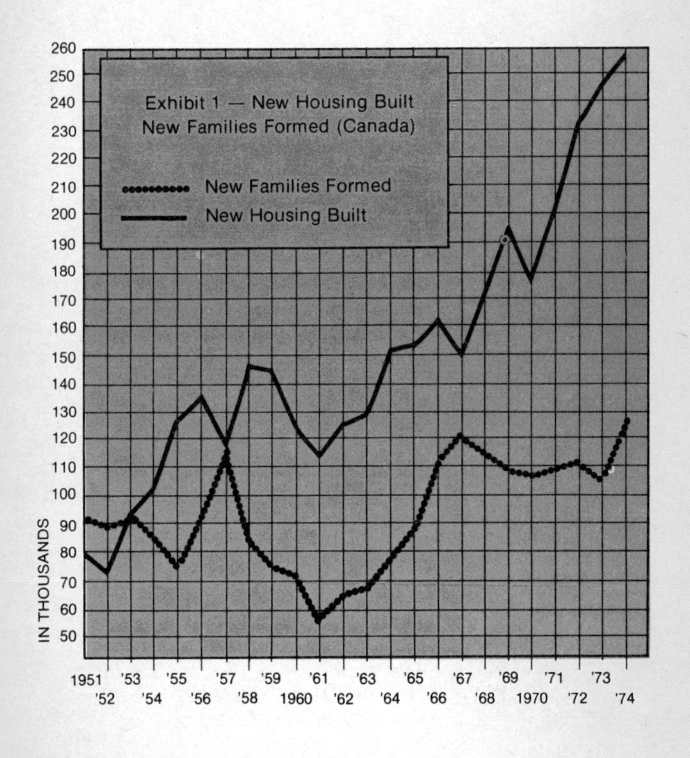

[2]L.B. Smith, Ibid. P. 19.

Exhibit 1 — New Housing Built,
New Families Formed (Canada)

	New Homes	New Families	New Households	New Houses per New Family	New Houses per New Household
1951	81,310	93,400		.87	
1952	73,087	89,800		.81	
1953	96,839	90,600		1.07	
1954	101,965	86,000		1.19	
1955	127,929	74,400		1.72	
1956	135,700	90,800	120,800	1.49	1.12
1957	117,283	116,600		1.00	
1958	146,686	83,300		1.76	
1959	145,671	76,800		1.90	
1960	123,757	71,300		1.74	
1961	115,608	56,500	100,600	1.76	1.15
1962	126,682	65,400		1.94	
1963	128,191	68,400		1.87	
1964	150,963	77,100		1.97	
1965	153,037	89,200		1.72	
1966	162,192	110,600	150,600	1.47	1.1
1967	149,242	120,600		1.24	
1968	170,993	114,500		1.49	
1969	195,826	108,500		1.80	
1970	175,827	107,700		1.63	
1971	201,232	108,600	163,600	1.85	1.2
1972	232,227	111,000		2.09	
1973	246,581	105,000		2.35	
1974	257,243	124,000	179,000	2.07	1.4

Sources: Central Mortgage and Housing — Canadian Housing Statistics (CMHC-CHS) 1973, Tables 121 and 117; 1974 Table 1.

There had been, by whatever measure, a steady trend toward improvement in the availability, quality and relative cost of housing during the twenty-year period ending 1969. With a growing population, the precondition for this improvement was new construction at an unprecedented rate.

The information contained in Exhibit 1 indicates that the trend in housing construction that was evident in 1970 continued at least until 1974. For example, in 1952, new housing units were being completed more slowly than new families were being formed. By 1974, this had been completely reversed and the number of housing completions was double the number of family formations.

If total households (which includes families, singles, communes, etc.) is used as the basis for determining the adequacy of housing construction, the improvement does not seem to be quite as dramatic, but is substantial nevertheless. In 1956, total housing construction was about equal to total household formation and by 1974, was exceeding household formation by about 40 per cent. (That is, for each 10 households formed 14 housing units were being completed).

Thus, on the basis of both these comparisons, it would appear that Canada is still producing more than enough housing to house additions to its population.

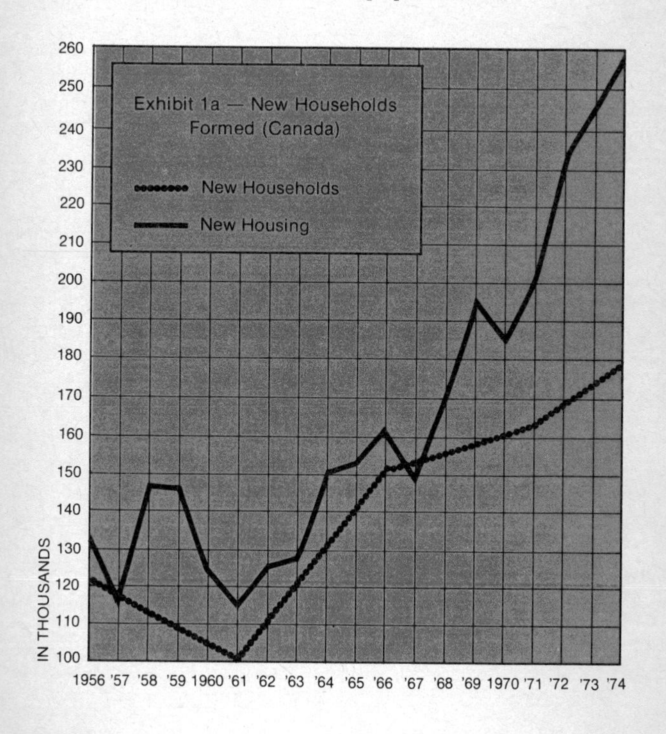

Living space

The results of this relative excess of housing production are reflected in the various measures of crowding[3] that are available. As Exhibit 2 shows, the increase in the number of homes available has permitted a substantial amount of "undoubling" of families. In 1951, more than one family in ten was not maintaining an independent home. By 1971, only one family in thirty was not maintaining a separate household. Furthermore, members of all households had more living space on average than was available in 1961.

Exhibit 2 — Doubling-Up of Families (Canada)

	Number of Families (thousands)	**Number Doubling Up (thousands)**	**Percentage of Total Families Doubling Up**
1951	3,025	321	10.6
1961	3,932	236	6.0
1971	4,925	172	3.5

Source: Central Mortgage and Housing, *Canadian Housing Statistics,* 1974, table 113.

Exhibit 3 contains information on the number of rooms per person in the average Canadian home. The statistics indicate that whereas in 1961 the average person had access to 1.4 rooms, by 1971 this had increased to 1.6 rooms. Although on the surface this does not seem to be much improvement, it does represent an increase of about 15 per cent in living space per person.

[3]"Crowding" statistics are essentially measures of living space per person. Given that most of the statistics for Canada indicate a complete absence of crowding, this is, perhaps, an infelicitous choice of terminology. It is, however, the conventional term.

Exhibit 3
Living Space
Number of Rooms per Person
in Canada

Household group	1961	1971
Average for all Canadian Households	1.4	1.6
Lowest Income Households	1.2	1.8
Second Lowest Income Households	1.3	1.6
Middle Income Households	1.3	1.6
Second Highest Income Households	1.4	1.6
Highest Income Households	1.7	1.9

More for low-income groups

The most interesting aspect of the "living space" data is the fact that the biggest improvement (from 1.2 to 1.8 rooms per person) has occurred where it was most necessary — namely, in the lowest income group. This increase of 50 per cent in the access of low-income households to living space is probably a consequence of the "filtering down" that occurs as the general standard of housing improves. That is, the relative excess of the construction of new housing (which is presumably occupied by the higher income households) over the rate of household formation makes available more housing for households with lower incomes.

Exhibit 3 — Living Space in Canada
(Number of Rooms per Person)

	1961	1971
Average for all Canadian Households	1.4	1.6
Average for Lowest Income Households	1.2	1.8
Average for Second Lowest Income Households	1.3	1.6
Average for Middle Income Households	1.3	1.6
Average for Second Highest Income Households	1.4	1.6
Average for Highest Income Households	1.7	1.9

Source: Economic Council of Canada, Eleventh Annual Review, *Economic Targets and Social Indicators,* Information Canada, Ottawa, 1974, P. 83. The data in this exhibit are reported as the reciprocal of the Economic Council's data.

Another interesting indicator of access to living space is the comparison of how much space the average Canadian has available relative to how much people in other countries have.

Exhibit 4 — International Comparison of Living Space
(Number of Rooms per Person)

Country	Year Measured	Average Number of Rooms per person
United Kingdom	1961	1.6
United States	1970	1.6
Canada	1961	1.4
	1971	1.6
Australia	1971	1.5
Sweden	1970	1.4
New Zealand	1966	1.3
Denmark	1965	1.3
France	1968	1.1
Japan	1970	1.0
Finland	1970	1.0

Exhibit 4 presents such an international comparison. Although the data for the different countries are not exactly comparable because the definition of "a room" varies from country to country, the broad impression conveyed by the numbers is clear. Canada ranks first with the U.S. and the U.K. in terms of access to living space. The average Canadian has access to roughly 60 per cent more living space than the average Finn or Japanese, while countries like Sweden and New Zealand provide access to living space comparable to what Canadians had in 1961.

Exhibit 4 — International Comparison of Living Space
(Number of Rooms per Person)

Country	Year Measured	Average Number of Rooms Per Person
United Kingdom	1961	1.6
United States	1970	1.6
Canada	(1961) 1971	(1.4) 1.6
Australia	1971	1.5
Sweden	1970	1.4
New Zealand	1966	1.3
Denmark	1965	1.3
France	1968	1.1
Japan	1970	1.0
Finland	1970	1.0

Source: Economic Council of Canada, Eleventh Annual Review, *Economic Targets and Social Indicators,* Information Canada, 1974, Page 75. Our data are presented as reciprocals of the data presented in the Council's Studies.

The good old days

Access to more living space does not in itself guarantee an improved standard of housing. An equally important factor is the quality of the living space. This particular aspect of housing is difficult to quantify on the average and this difficulty leads analysts to use information that might implicitly give an indication of quality. One set of such information is the data collected on the standard of amenities associated with living space in Canada. Exhibit 5 displays information on this implicit "quality" index.

Exhibit 5 indicates that there has been a substantial increase in the average standard of amenities associated with the housing stock and hence, an overall increase in the quality. The facts that roughly one in two Canadian households did not have piped hot and cold water; that one in three lacked bathing facilities and indoor toilet facilities as late as 1951 are sobering reminders of the extent to which the level of convenience associated with Canadian housing has changed. In 1974 it is difficult to find a housing unit that does not incorporate these "basic" amenities. (Only about 4 per cent lack bath and piped hot and cold water).

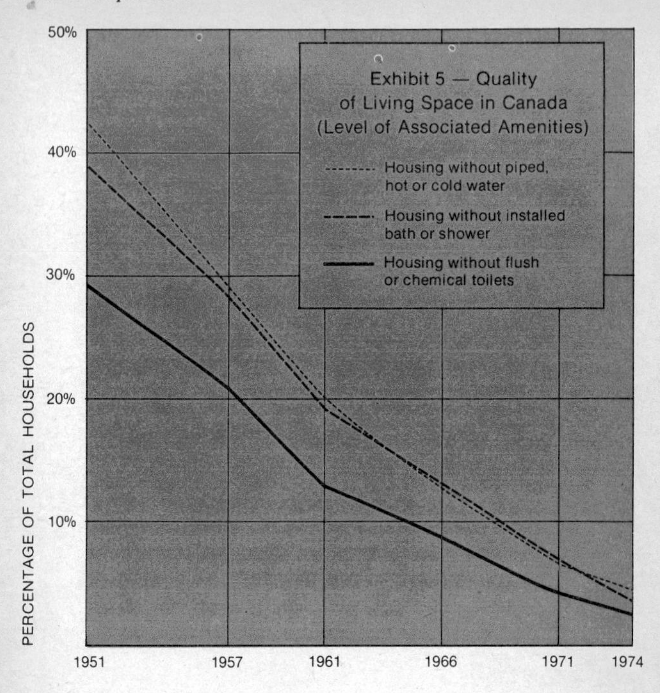

Exhibit 5 — Quality of Living Space in Canada
(Level of Associated Amenities)

	Percentage of Total Households		
	Without flush or chemical toilets	**Without piped hot and cold water**	**Without installed bath or shower**
1951	29.3	43.1	39.2
1957	20.4	28.9	28.5
1961	12.8	19.8	19.1
1966	8.4	12.6	12.8
1971	4.0	6.5	6.6
1974	2.3	4.3	3.8

Source: Central Mortgage and Housing Corporation, *Canadian Housing Statistics*, 1974, Page 87.

Thus, not only has the access of every Canadian to "living space" increased since 1961 and since the Smith report was written, but the quality of this living space has improved as well.

Smith's third conclusion in 1970:

> 'To the extent that shelter costs are not outpacing and are probably lagging income increases so that housing accommodations are generally more affordable, there is no housing problem.'[4]

Conditions with respect to Smith's third conclusion have changed somewhat since 1970, as Exhibit 6 shows. Whereas the overall increase in the cost of living was about 16.8 per cent over the five-year period ending in 1969, it rose by 28.6 per cent during the five-year period ending in 1974. On the other hand, personal disposable income which had risen by 40.4 per cent from 1965 to 1969 increased by 59.4 per cent. The relatively smaller increase in the growth in income, combined with a faster rate of growth of prices, has meant that the rate of growth of the real standard of living of Canadians has been slower in the past five years than it was in the five years that preceded Smith's study.

Rents a bargain?

Although the standard of living of Canadians has improved more slowly in recent times than in the past, there appears to have been a relative reduction in the cost of accommodation — at least for tenants. According to the rental index presented in Exhibit 6, the cost of rental accommodation increased by 14.1 per cent from 1965 to 1969, while the increase from 1970 to 1974 was only 8.14 per cent. Homeowners have not, in general, been as fortunate as tenants. During the period 1970 to 1974, the costs of accommodation to homeowners rose by 40.8 per cent as compared to 28.9 per cent over the period 1965 to 1969.

[4]L.B. Smith, Op. Cit. P. 19.

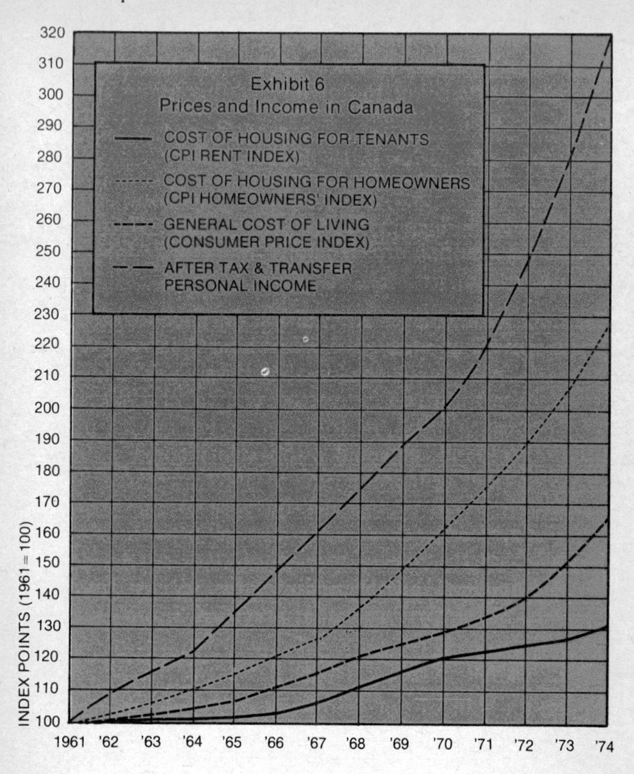

Comment: Owing to a bias in the sampling technique employed by Statistics Canada, the shelter cost for tenants is probably underestimated by the shelter cost index. However, in order to reverse the conclusions about tenant and home-owner costs, the bias would have to be in the order of 70 per cent — i.e. rents would have to be nearly twice as high as Statistics Canada says they are and grow three times faster than the index indicates. It is less difficult to accept the index as it is than to accept that the bias could be that large.

Exhibit 6 — Prices and Income in Canada

	Cost of Housing: For Tenants (CPI Rent Index)	For Home-owners (CPI Home-owners Index)	General Cost of Living	Total Personal Incomes	Effective Income Tax Rate	After Tax (and Transfer) Personal Incomes
1961	100.0	100.0	100.0	100.0	10.6	100.0
1962	100.2	102.8	101.2	108.9	10.5	109.1
1963	100.3	105.9	103.0	115.7	10.5	115.8
1964	101.2	110.4	104.8	123.8	11.4	122.8
1965	101.9	115.0	107.4	136.4	11.7	134.8
1966	103.6	120.1	111.4	153.1	13.4	148.3
1967	107.1	126.9	115.4	168.0	14.7	160.3
1968	111.8	136.1	120.1	184.9	15.9	174.0
1969	116.3	148.3	125.5	205.3	17.7	189.2
1970	120.3	161.3	129.7	221.0	18.9	200.7
1971	122.5	174.3	133.4	244.6	19.2	221.1
1972	124.3	188.3	139.8	273.9	19.0	248.1
1973	126.4	207.0	150.4	312.2	19.2	282.4
1974	130.1	227.1	166.8	355.1	19.9	320.0
Increase 1961-1974	30.1%	127.1%	66.8%	255.1%	87.7%	220.0%

Sources: Central Mortgage and Housing — *Canadian Housing Statistics,* 1974, Tables 106, 102.

National Income and Expenditure Accounts, Statistics Canada, Various years, to 1974.

Less income spent on shelter

The most recently available information (1972) indicates that the net effect of rising incomes and rising costs of accommodation has been to stabilize the percentage of income spent on shelter. The trend from 1962 to 1969 had been toward a reduction in the percentage of income spent on shelter — the average falling from 18.6 to 16.0 per cent. From 1969 to 1972 the increase was one-tenth of one per cent on average for Canadians. The most important factor working to reduce the proportion of income spent on shelter (as is evident from Exhibit 7) is the fact that the average income of Canadians has been rising very quickly and there are, accordingly, fewer people at a subsistence level of income. In 1969, for example, 16.9 per cent of all Canadians had incomes of $4,000 or less. In 1972, only 13.3 per cent had incomes that low and so, even though shelter took a bigger portion of a person's income in 1972 if their income was less than $4,000, there were fewer people affected. In fact, whereas in 1969 64.4 per cent of Canadians paid out more than 18 per cent of their income to obtain shelter, by 1972 about 62 per cent paid less than 16 per cent.

Exhibit 7 — Percentage of Income Spent on Shelter (Canada)

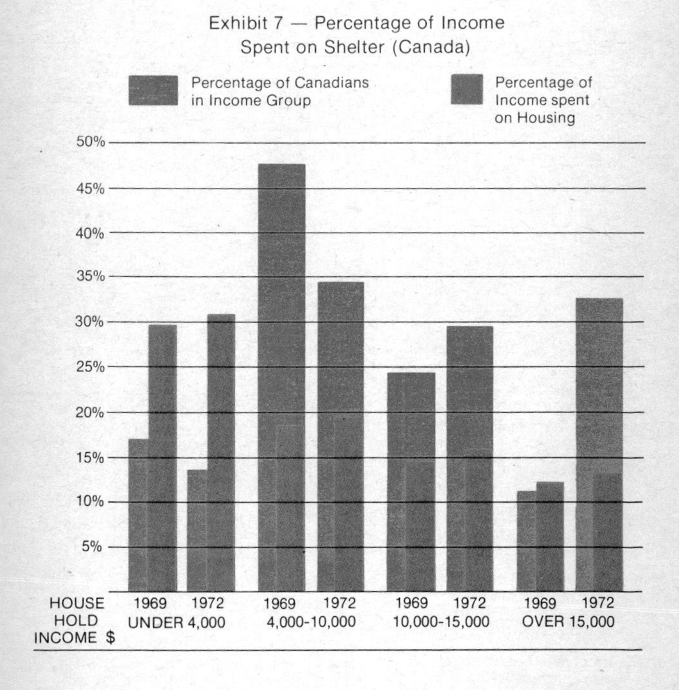

Exhibit 7 — Percentage of Income Spent on Shelter (Canada)

	1962	1969	1972
By all income groups	18.6	16.0	16.1
Percentage of Canadians	(100.0)	(100.0)	(100.0)
By households with income under $4,000		29.9	30.7
Percentage of Canadians with income under $4,000		(16.9)	(13.3)
By households with income between $4,000 and $10,000		18.3	19.8
Percentage of Canadians with income between $4,000 and $10,000		(47.5)	(34.7)
By households with income between $10,000 and $15,000		14.9	15.8
Percentage of Canadians with income between $10,000 and $15,000		(24.5)	(29.7)
By households with income over $15,000		12.4	13.2
Percentage of Canadians with income over $15,000		(11.0)	(32.3)

Source: Statistics Canada, *Family Expenditure in Canada,* Volume III, Information Canada, 1969. Table II.

Statistics Canada, *Urban Family Expenditure,* 1972, Selected tables. Page 18.

There is a rule of thumb that a person should spend, say, 20-25 per cent of their income on rents or principal, interest and taxes. Since this rule is apparently in wide spread use, the average of 16.1 per cent of income spent on shelter appears to be very low. A reconciliation of the difference is possible along the following lines.

The 25 per cent rule of thumb applies to home purchasers at the time that they buy their houses. During subsequent years, their incomes typically rise much faster than the principal, interest and tax payments they have to make. On average, half of the total number of homeowners will be half way through the term of their mortgage, i.e. about 12 years will have elapsed. If we assume that during that period the increase in incomes is, on average, twice as great as the increase in the costs of "carrying the house" (an assumption that is in keeping with the information in Exhibit 6), then the average percentage of income spent by homeowners would be expected to fall to about 13 per cent. Since homeowners comprise more than 60 per cent of total families, this would produce an average shelter cost-to-income ratio (including tenants) of about 16 per cent.

"The cost-expense-rent squeeze"

The cost of rental accommodation index (Exhibit 6) indicates that, relative to other things consumers buy (the Consumer Price Index) and relative to homeownership costs (the homeownership index), rented accommodation is a bargain for tenants. However, to the extent that landlords experience the same sort of costs as homeowners, it is clear that tenants cannot continue to enjoy their present position. In fact, investment in rental property has become increasingly unprofitable — a trend which Smith clearly identified in 1970.

> "Recent events suggest that further housing problems may be facing us within the apartment market itself . . . and over the next few years this can be expected to continue unless rents rise sharply. This distortion can be called a cost-expense-rent squeeze.
>
> Most of the points clearly indicate the tremendous cost pressures arising to drive up rents and/or curtail construction.
>
> In today's political environment, however, rising rents will generate intensified pressure for rent control or rental review boards and increasingly stringent regulations for the landlord which could make new construction a very hazardous undertaking."[5]

Things have not improved much in recent times, as is indicated by the data presented in Exhibit 6. The cost-expense-rent squeeze that Smith identified has continued.

[5]L.B. Smith, Op. Cit., Pages 16-18.

A particularly graphic indication of the extent of the squeeze is to be found in a detailed study of the Vancouver housing market conducted by Professor J.G. Cragg, of the University of British Columbia Department of Economics, in 1974. This study was commissioned by the British Columbia Rentalsman to determine what the Allowable Rent Increase ought to be under the Province of British Columbia's rent control legislation. Professor Cragg determined that:

> "An Allowable Rent Increase of 30% would cover completely the past changes in costs . . . An . . . increase of 16% is probably a lower bound on the feasible operation of rent control . . . an increase of still smaller magnitude if effective, can be expected to entail very strong dangers that the usually cited undesirable effects of rent control will begin to emerge and that new rental construction will not occur."[6]

In its wisdom, the Government of British Columbia allowed an increase of only 10.6 per cent. This increase is less than one-third the increase necessary to cover "completely the past changes in costs" and only two-thirds as large as the rate that Cragg suggested as the absolute minimum.

Singleminded policy

The 'coup de grace' to the profitability of rental housing was delivered in 1971 in the form of Finance Minister Benson's tax reform measures.[7] We have just seen that Smith was arguing strongly in 1971 that investment in rental accommodation simply was not feasible. The tax provisions that were introduced in 1971 had the effect of making such investments even less profitable and even less attractive to investors. In the light of Smith's warnings, the 1971 change in the tax act appears, retrospectively, to have been a policy measure out of keeping with responsible action. It is even

[6] J.G. Cragg, "Rent Control Report" submitted to the British Columbia Rentalsman. Mimeo, 1974.

[7] *Summary of 1971 Tax Reform Legislation,* Honourable E.J. Benson, Minister of Finance, Department of Finance, Ottawa, 1971.

more difficult to understand when one takes into account the warnings (in 1966) contained in the Carter Report which was the source document for the Benson White Paper on Tax Reform and, ultimately, the source of the change in legislation.

In his report, Carter clearly warned that if the proposed tax measure was adopted,

> "construction activity would be reduced for a period until rents rose sufficiently in response to a growing demand to restore the relative attractiveness of real estate investments . . . the government would probably have to take action to offset any reduction in apartment construction during the transitional period."[8]

Of course, the required increase in rents did not materialize, the required government construction did not occur and in 1975, the Finance Minister was forced to "temporarily" suspend parts of the tax measure that had been so single-mindedly installed in 1971.

A perfectly predictable "emergency situation"

It is always difficult to disentangle and quantify the separate effects that government policy and other developments have on a particular aspect of the economy and, although in this respect the housing market is no exception, it is clear that the housing market condition in Canada in 1975 bears a depressing resemblance to that forecast by Smith in 1970 and anticipated by Carter as early as 1966. The market has certainly reacted to the "cost-expense-rent squeeze" and the hostility of the political climate in exactly the way that Smith projected. The total number of new apartments being constructed in Canada has fallen dramatically during the four years since Smith issued his warning.

Exhibit 8 displays the extent of new apartment construction over the period 1961 - 1974. In order to remove the effect that monetary policy has on all construction activity we display apartment "starts" relative to total starts. (Total starts includes single houses, duplex and apartment starts).

[8]Report of the Royal Commission on Taxation, Volume 6, Queen's Printer, Ottawa 1966. Page 128.

We also display apartment completions relative to total completions and the vacancy rate — the latter being a rough measure of the supply of apartments relative to the demand.

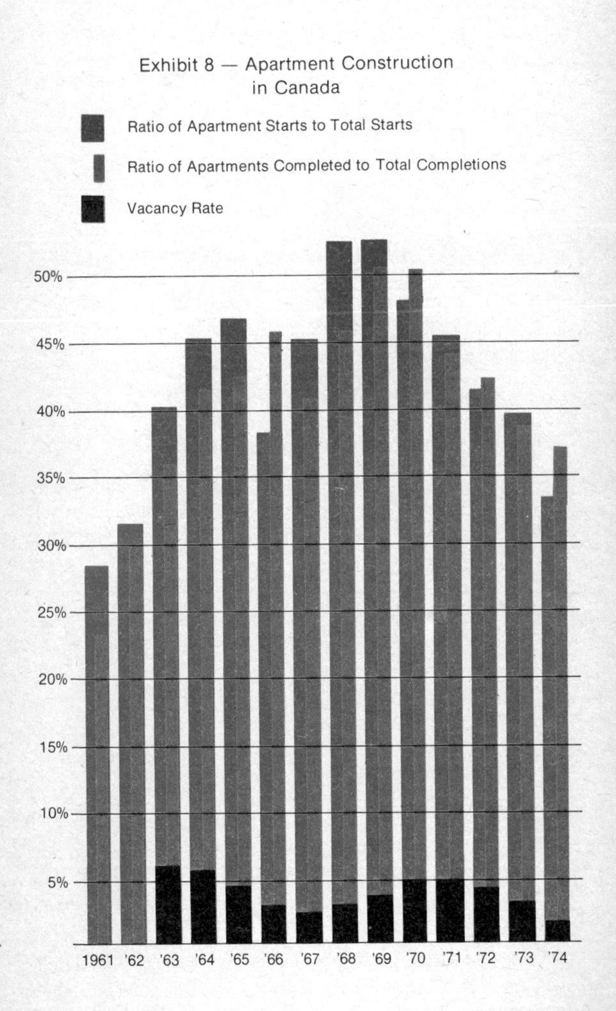

Exhibit 8 — Apartment Construction in Canada

	Ratio of Apartment Starts to Total "Starts"	Ratio of Apartments Completed to Total Completions*	Vacancy Rate
1961	28.4%	23.2%	—
1962	31.5%	30.0%	—
1963	40.2%	35.9%	6.1%
1964	45.3%	41.6%	5.7%
1965	46.8%	42.5%	4.6%
1966	38.3%	45.8%	3.2%
1967	45.2%	40.9%	1.4%
1968	52.5%	45.8%	2.7%
1969	52.7%	50.5%	4.0%
1970	48.2%	50.4%	5.0%
1971	45.4%	44.2%	5.0%
1972	41.5%	42.3%	4.5%
1973	39.6%	38.8%	3.4%
1974	33.3%	37.2%	1.8%

Source: Central Mortgage and Housing Corporation; *Canadian Housing Statistics*, 1970, 1973, 1974. Vacancy rates not available prior to 1963.

*It should be noted that for various reasons not all "starts" get "completed" and accordingly there is no exact correspondence between the starts ratio and the completions ratio.

Several things seem clear from this information. First, apartment construction has fallen precipitously in relative terms since 1970. Second, the measured vacancy rate rises and falls as apartment completions rise and fall. Third, the relative number of apartment completions in 1975 will fall to a level lower than it has been since 1963. Fourth, vacancy rates will likely continue to fall and will remain at a low level until either apartment construction has resumed or until the demand for existing suites is brought into balance with the supply. Neither of these things will occur until rents rise.

End of an era

Accordingly, although tenants have been relatively more fortunate than homeowners in the recent past, this advantage has, to some extent, sown the seeds for a reversal in the future. The fact that rents have not risen has led to reduced construction and this, in turn, has produced a tighter housing market. Rents will eventually rise, unless prevented from doing so by political intervention, until rental accommodation reflects the true cost structure that landlords face. In this event, the relative advantage that tenants now enjoy will be removed.

The real danger for the Canadian housing market is the possibility that rents will not be allowed to adjust to an economically viable level. And, as the British Columbia Government's treatment of the Cragg report indicated, there may not be a political willingness to accept developments in the short run that are inevitable if the housing standard of Canadians is to continue to improve in the long run.

IS THERE A HOUSING PROBLEM?

Much of the current public debate on housing seems to have imbedded in it the presumption that there is, if not a housing crisis, then at least a housing shortage. Moreover, the clamour that "the government should do something" about the current "state of affairs" is mounting in virtually every province in Canada. The current campaigns by tenants for rent control are an aspect of this activity. But, is there a housing problem?

The foregoing analysis of the data available suggests, surprising though it will seem to some readers, that there is no housing problem. That is, there is no housing problem in the sense that the *housing market* is in a state of malfunction. To this extent our conclusion echoes that of the authors of *The Real Poverty Report"*, who concluded:

> "The problem is probably *not* that there are not enough decent houses to go around "[9]

The conclusion that there is no general housing problem is no less sensible now than when *The Real Poverty Report* was written.

[9] *The Real Poverty Report,* Ian Adams, William Cameron, Brian Hill and Peter Penz, M.G. Hurtig Ltd., Edmonton, 1971, Page 76.

No symptoms

Put another way, if there is a housing problem, what are its symptoms? For example, does the fact that the average Canadian occupies a quantity and quality of living space unsurpassed in the world suggest that Canada has a housing shortage of crisis proportions? Or, can housing be considered too expensive for the average person to afford when Canadian families, on average, spend more of their income on recreation, alcohol, tobacco and automobiles than they do on shelter?

Of course, Canadians are spending more on housing in 1975 than they did in 1961, but that is not surprising given the enormous improvement in the quality and quantity of space that the average Canadian occupies. Furthermore, since 1961, the proportion of income that Canadians spend on shelter has *fallen* by nearly three percentage points. (In 1961, the average Canadian spent 18.6 per cent of income on shelter; by 1972, this had fallen to 16.1 per cent). So, in relative terms, Canadians are getting more (housing) for less (income) in 1975 than they got in 1961.

The problem is poverty

There is no housing problem — but there is a problem. The nature of the problem is well illustrated in the following quotes from a book "about rent control . . . and how tenants can organize to win and enforce it".[10]

> "Even if you can't get good statistics, it's often helpful to publicize specific cases of families paying a large portion of their incomes for rent[11] . . . Stories about specific families who are suffering from the housing crisis . . . can be very useful in bringing statistics to life, and in getting publicity for the rent control campaign."[12]

The concern that lies behind these well-intentioned, though misdirected, remarks is the same concern that motivated the conclusions of *The Real Poverty Report:*

[10]Emily Achtenburg, *Less Rent More Control;* Urban Planning Aid Inc., Cambridge, Mass. 1973. Page 2.

[11]Ibid., Page 29.

[12]Ibid., Page 27.

> "The problem is probably not that there are not enough decent homes to go around; the problem is that the poor do not have enough money either to rent or to buy them".[13]

The problem, quite simply, is that some Canadians do not have sufficient income. Unlike Ms. Achtenburg, the authors of *The Real Poverty Report* concluded that if "the poor" cannot afford adequate housing then the solution is to raise their incomes. Of course, to some extent this occurs as a natural consequence of a rising general standard of living and in the end it is this rising standard of general affluence that will eliminate poverty. For example, in Canada, between 1969 and 1972, the number of families with incomes over $10,000 increased from 35.5 per cent to 62 per cent of the total, while the number that had incomes below $4,000 fell by 3.6 percentage points to 13.3 per cent of the total. But, there is still a fairly substantial number of Canadians for whom the provision of basic necessities is a problem.

In large measure, social concerns about housing are, in effect, concerns about this inadequacy of the income of certain segments of the population; that is, lack of income, together with rising prices of necessities, inflicts hardship. The policies that are enacted to deal with these concerns should, therefore, be directed at this basic income problem.

Rent control — the solution?

If poverty is the problem, can rent control be relied upon to solve it, or is rent control part of the problem? Rent control is an attempt to deal with the poverty problem by intervening in the market for housing. So, in order to assess its usefulness as a policy instrument, one must answer two fundamental questions. First, is rent control an efficient way to provide the poor with an income supplement? Second, does rent control have long-term effects on the housing market that offset its short-term benefits for tenants?

The essays in the second part of this volume deal specifically with these points and the results point unambiguously to the conclusion that, quite apart from being a "cure" for any problem, rent control quickly becomes a major

[13] *The Real Poverty Report*, op. cit. Page 76.

cause of the "disease". The reader is referred to the article by Professor Olsen on the question of rent control as aid to the poor and to all of the articles in Part II for an historical and geographical survey of the evidence on the housing market side-effects of rent control.

SUMMARY — WHAT ARE THE FACTS?

Housing Facts

1. Housing construction in Canada has exceeded family and household formation in each year for the past 20 years.

2. In 1951 more than one family in ten was not maintaining a separate household. In 1975 less than one family in thirty is not maintaining a separate household.

3. Canadians, on average, have access to 1.6 rooms per person, an increase of 15 per cent since 1961, and enjoy a quality and quantity of housing unsurpassed in the world.

4. While in 1951, 43 per cent of Canadian homes were without piped hot and cold running water this has dropped to 4 per cent in 1974.

5. During the 5-year period 1965 to 1969 the cost of rental accommodation rose by 14.1 per cent. In the most recent 5-year period (1970-1974) the increase was only 8.14 per cent. During the same period homeownership costs rose 40.8 per cent as compared with 28.9 per cent in the 1965-1969 period.

6. Since 1961 personal disposable income has risen by 220 per cent whereas rents have risen only 30 per cent, homeownership costs by 127 per cent and the general cost of living 67 per cent.

7. The latest information available indicates that shelter expenditures absorb about 16 per cent of the average Canadian family's income whereas in 1962 the percentage was nearly 19 per cent. The same data indicates that the average Canadian family spends more on recreation, tobacco, alcohol and automobiles than it does on shelter.

8. Housing conditions that prevail in 1975 were perfectly foreseen and documented in a government study in 1970 and anticipated by a Royal Commission as early as 1966.

9. The proportion of apartment construction out of total residential construction will fall to a lower level in 1975 than it has been since 1962.

10. Rents will have to rise in the future to offset increases in costs and changes in Federal Tax legislation.

Conclusions

1. There is no housing problem for the average Canadian.

2. The problem, in the words of *The Real Poverty Report,*

   "is not that there are not enough decent houses to go around; the problem is that the poor do not have enough money either to rent or to buy them."

3. The solution to this "housing problem" is probably not to be found in a further round of interventions in the housing market.

APPENDIX A

REMARKS ON APPARENT INCONSISTENCIES IN PUBLISHED INFORMATION ABOUT HOUSING COSTS

Periodically, Statistics Canada conducts a survey of household expenditure in Canada to determine, among other things, what percentage of their incomes Canadians spend on housing. The results of this survey are compiled by income group and by class of tenure — i.e. whether the accommodation is owned or rented. The recent results of

Exhibit A1 — Percentage of Income Spent on Shelter by Tenants and Homeowners in Canada

Year	Overall Average	Average for Homeowners	Average for Tenants
1962	18.6	15.7	18.3
1964	16.8	15.1	17.4
1969	16.0	15.1	17.4
1972	16.1	14.7	17.9

Source: Statistics Canada, *Family Expenditure in Canada*, Information Canada, 1969.

Statistics Canada, *Urban Family Expenditure*, 1972, Selected tables, Mimeo, Statistics Canada.

Statistics Canada, *Urban Family Expenditure*, 1962, 1964, Queen's Printer, Ottawa.

this survey (1972) indicate (Exhibit A1) that at the time of the survey tenants were paying a higher fraction (17.9%) of their incomes for shelter than they had at the time of the previous survey (1969). Furthermore, according to the 1972 data, homeowners were devoting less of their income to shelter costs than they had in 1969. This information apparently conflicts with the costs of rental accommodation index reported in Exhibit 6 in the text. (Reproduced here as Exhibit A2 for reader convenience). The purpose of this appendix is to attempt to resolve this conflict.

The rental cost index is calculated from information gathered in the Labour Force Survey. In constructing the index, Statistics Canada makes an effort to adjust the rents paid for changes in quality and quantity of housing services purchased. Accordingly, it is a measure of the cost of "standardized" accommodation and is roughly comparable on a year-to-year basis.

Exhibit A2 — Prices and Income in Canada

	Cost of Housing:					
	For Tenants (CPI Rent Index)	**For Home-owners (CPI Home-owners index)**	**General Cost of Living**	**Total Personal Incomes**	**Effective Income Tax Rate**	**After Tax (and Transfer) Personal Incomes**
1961	100.0	100.0	100.0	100.0	10.6	100.0
1962	100.2	102.8	101.2	108.9	10.5	109.1
1963	100.3	105.9	103.0	115.7	10.5	115.8
1964	101.2	110.4	104.8	123.8	11.4	122.8
1965	101.9	115.0	107.4	136.4	11.7	134.8
1966	103.6	120.1	111.4	153.1	13.4	148.3
1967	107.1	126.9	115.4	168.0	14.7	160.3
1968	111.8	136.1	120.1	184.9	15.9	174.0
1969	116.3	148.3	125.5	205.3	17.7	189.2
1970	120.3	161.3	129.7	221.0	18.9	200.7
1971	122.5	174.3	133.4	244.6	19.2	221.1
1972	124.3	188.3	139.8	273.9	19.0	248.1
1973	126.4	207.0	150.4	312.2	19.2	282.4
1974	130.1	227.1	166.8	355.1	19.9	320.0
Increase 1961-1974	30.1%	127.1%	66.8%	255.1%	87.7%	220.0%

Sources: Central Mortgage and Housing — *Canadian Housing Statistics*, 1974, Tables 106, 102.

National Income and Expenditure Accounts, Statistics Canada, Various years, to 1974.

The percentage of income spent on shelter as calculated from the Family Expenditure Survey, on the other hand, does not take account of changes in either the quantity or quality of space occupied. Accordingly, the fraction of income spent on shelter is not, strictly speaking, a very good measure of the change in the cost of shelter on a year-to-year basis. For example, if neither a family's income nor the cost of apartments changed from one year to the next, but a family moved from a one-bedroom to a two-bedroom apartment, then the percentage of income spent on shelter would increase. In this case, the increase would be indicating the fact that the family occupied more space, and not that the cost of apartments had changed.

A situation similar to that outlined in the foregoing example seems to have arisen in Canada. We know that homeowners' shelter costs have risen much more quickly than the shelter costs of tenants. (Exhibit A2). In spite of this, the fraction of income spent on shelter by homeowners has fallen slightly while the fraction of income spent by tenants has risen. At least a partial explanation for this is to be found in Exhibit A3 which records, in rough terms, the amount of living space occupied by tenants and homeowners.

Exhibit A3 — Living Space in Owned and Rented Premises

	Owned		Rented	
	1966	**1971**	**1966**	**1971**
Percentage of total households with:				
More than 2 rooms per person	27.6	30.4	20.8	27.7
Between 1 and 2 rooms per person	60.0	60.3	65.1	63.5
Less than 1 room per person	12.4	9.3	14.1	8.8
TOTALS	100.0	100.0	100.0	100.0

Source: Perspective Canada, Statistics Canada, 11-507, Information Canada, 1974, Page 216.

According to this census information, tenants have increased the amount of space that they occupy much more than have homeowners. Between 1966 and 1971 there was a six per cent increase in the number of tenant households occupying living space with more than one room per person. During the same period the number of homeowner households occupying (on average) more than one room per person increased by only three per cent. Thus, although homeowners on average occupy more space than tenants, the rate at which their access to space is increasing is much lower than it is for tenants.

In other words, on average, more tenants are moving into larger accommodation and, accordingly, the percentage of income that tenants spend on accommodation would have increased even in the absence of changes in incomes or the cost of accommodation.

Information that confirms the impression that tenants are occupying more space is to be found in Exhibit 3. That information indicates that lower-income families have increased their access to living space by about 50 per cent during the interval between the 1961 and 1971 censuses, whereas the average increase for all Canadians was only 15 per cent. If one assumes that low-income families are largely tenants, then this information confirms the impression that tenants are, on average, increasing the amount of space they occupy faster than homeowners are.

APPENDIX B

A COMMENT ON THE ECONOMIC COUNCIL'S "COST OF HOUSING" INDICATOR

In its *Eleventh Annual Review,* the Economic Council of Canada constructed a rent-to-income ratio as an indicator of the cost of housing. That is, they calculated the average rent per room and divided that by household income to get a measure of the cost of accommodation. According to their calculations, rent per room as a percentage of total household income rose from 3.7 per cent in 1961 to 4.2 per cent in 1971.[1] Since this piece of information conflicts with the information provided by the Statistics Canada survey of shelter costs presented in Exhibit 7 (in the text), we will devote some time to a consideration of the Economic Council's measure.

In order to calculate a rent-to-income ratio for all families, it is necessary to regard all families as tenants, i.e., owner-occupiers are regarded as both landlord and tenant. In making their calculation of rent for owner-occupiers, the Economic Council apparently[2] assumed that rent was equal to one per cent of total house value. So, if at the time the census was conducted a family was occupying a house valued at $20,000, their rent was "imputed" as $200 per month. Of course, the amount that the family actually paid in principal, interest, taxes, maintenance, etc. could have been quite different than this estimate. On average one would expect an estimate of rent calculated in this way to be an overestimate of actual cash rent because house values have risen more quickly than costs of maintenance.

[1]Economic Council of Canada, Eleventh Annual Review, *Economic Targets and Social Indicators,* Information Canada, 1974, Page 87.

[2]Eleventh Annual Review, Appendix A., Page 204, Footnote 2.

If, on the other hand, "imputed" rent and not cash rent is the outcome of their measure, an estimate of the percentage of income spent on rent calculated in the way that they suggest would be biased because the income measure used is incorrect. In order to demonstrate why this is so we have constructed a hypothetical example of a home-owning family.

Exhibit B1

	1961	**1971**
House Value	$10,000	$20,000
(of which equity)	$ 1,000	$13,000*
Rent Imputed	$100 per month	$200 per month
(Economic Council Basis)	$20 per room	$40 per room
Family Income (measured by Statistics Canada and used by the Economic Council)	$541 per month	$952 per month
Family Income (including imputed income from equity at 7%)	$547 per month	$1,028 per month
Rent (per room) as a percentage of measured income	3.7%	4.2%
Rent (per room) as a percentage of total income	3.7%	3.9%

*Of which $10,000 is assumed to be capital gain and $2,000 is assumed to be reduction in mortgage principal.

The example is presented in Exhibit B1. In the example I have assumed that the family bought and owned a 5-room house in 1961 that was valued at $10,000 and that they had an income of $6,486. Using the Economic Council's formula, the family's "imputed" rent in 1961 was $100 per month. This yields 3.7 per cent of monthly income as the cost per room. The measured family income used in that calculation ignores, as most families do, the fact that the family had implicit income from their equity in the house. In other words, the down payment of $1,000 could have been invested in an asset other than a house and the family's measured income would have been higher by the amount of interest. (In imputing the income on the down payment and on accumulated equity in the example, an interest rate of 7% has been used). Since the Economic Council's formula includes this interest income foregone as part of the "rent" of owner-occupied dwellings, the corresponding income must also be imputed.

Although allowance for "imputed income" makes no difference to the calculation in the initial year (1961) because of rounding, the difference for 1971 is quite dramatic. The calculation done with measured income produces the Council's figure of 4.2 per cent, whereas the calculation done with total (including imputed) income is 3.9 per cent.

The conclusion that this example suggests is that to the extent that homeowners have equity in their homes, the procedure used by the Economic Council of Canada to calculate the rent-to-income ratio is biased. The extent of the bias depends on the extent to which families who own their own homes have equity in their homes.

Quite apart from this demonstration that the Council's measure *could be* biased, it is difficult to accept their estimate given the actual survey data presented in Exhibit 7 in the text and given the fact that the Council agrees that access to living space has increased. The survey data indicate a decline in the average proportion of income spent on shelter[3] from 1962 to 1972 of 2.5 percentage points. The "living space" data (Exhibit 3 in the text) indicate an increase in the average number of rooms per person. The shelter cost data indicate a reduction in the proportion of income spent on shelter. How, then, can it be said that the proportion of income spent per room has increased?

Since this particular "Social Indicator" will doubtless be the subject of much attention in the following decade one hopes that these apparent defects in its construction will be remedied.

[3]Shelter includes rent of premises and heat and light. The heat and light component has fallen slightly but not by enough to influence the overall conclusion that we have drawn with respect to the Economic Council's measure of premises costs as a proportion of income.

What are the Concepts?

M.A. WALKER
Chief Economist, The Fraser Institute

Rent control is a form of price fixing that increases the shortage of housing and ultimately reduces the ability of tenants to choose where and under what conditions they live.

Rent control is a form of tenant protection adopted because housing is a basic need like sunshine and fresh air and its provision ought not to be left to the vagaries of the market-place.

Not surprisingly, what rent control *seems* to be depends on your point of view. Whatever else rent control is, it is certainly an aspect of economic policy, and in the end will have effects that depend on peoples' economic behaviour. Rent control, as an aspect of social legislation, cannot avoid the reality that it is, in essence, a form of price control. Therefore, by definition, it creates (or exacerbates) a shortage of housing by increasing the quantity of housing demanded and decreasing the quantity of housing supplied.

This introductory essay provides a framework for the analysis of rent control from the economist's point of view. What *is* the economic behaviour of citizens as regards housing? What *is* a housing shortage? How *are* rents determined? What *are* price controls and what effects *do* they have in the short term and in the long term?

I THE DEMAND FOR HOUSING 'SERVICES'

What are we talking about?

Some of the confusion that surrounds the discussion of housing market operations arises because a general agreement is not reached by the discussants about the nature of the commodity that is being bought and sold. So, let's first consider the notion of housing as a consumer product.[1]

Houses and apartments are, in general, demanded because of the services that they provide to the occupant. For instance, housing units provide shelter, privacy and sanitary and other amenities. They also provide a source of recreation for some people and the facility to support other activities. The demand for houses or apartments is, accordingly, an expression of *"the demand for the services"* that housing units provide.

Basic shelter

The most basic level of housing service (and the one that is normally implied in statements of the sort, "every Canadian has the right to decent accommodation") is the shelter provided by housing. Such statements are ambiguous because the notion of "basic accommodation" is itself somewhat elusive and is very much tied in with the notion of standard of living and quality of life.[2] As the general level of affluence and social norms change, the perception of "basic accommodation" will also change. For this reason, it will always be somewhat difficult for society in general and people in particular to determine objectively what the basic shelter service of housing is.[3]

[1]A similar discussion, though more technical, is to be found in Richard R. Muth's essay, "The Demand for Non-Farm Housing", in *The Demand for Durable Goods,* Edited by Arnold C. Harberger, University of Chicago Press, 1960.

[2]For instance, does "basic accommodation" include piped running water, exclusive use of bath and exclusive use of a flush toilet? The answer for Canada in 1975 is an unqualified "yes"; the answer in 1951, when 43 per cent of Canadian households lacked piped water, 39 per cent lacked exclusive use of bath and 29 per cent lacked exclusive use of a flush toilet would probably have been "no". (See footnote 7.)

[3]The notion of basic shelter and the notion of "minimum standards" as set by local building codes and planning by-laws are not distinct. It is difficult to know whether affluence "pulls up" minimum standards or whether they are separate influences on the level of accommodation that is considered basic.

Very few housing units in the private sector are built as basic shelter. The vast majority are built as basic shelter *plus* some level of convenience or extra amenities. It is largely on the basis of the quantity of the latter that the price or rent is established. This is because the extras yield a flow of services to the occupant, either in the form of direct convenience or in the form of social prestige. The level of services provided by a given housing unit usually *falls* as the unit gets older, *rises* as renovations are made and *varies* as external factors such as neighbourhood conditions change. (Freeways are a modern example of such external factors). A given housing unit is thus capable of producing a varying amount of housing services.

To take a common-place example: the decision of a landlord to paint or wallpaper a room actually constitutes a decision *to increase the flow of housing services from a given housing unit.* Although this may be difficult to accept at first sight, the truth of it can be quickly seen in the fact that a newly-painted apartment attracts a higher rent than an identical one that has not been decorated.

Wants and the law of demand

The desire to have access to housing is one of an almost unlimited number of human "wants". The process by which *wants are satisfied* constitutes the general subject matter of economics. The *want* for housing services becomes the *demand* for housing services as soon as an individual has made a *choice* to spend some of his income to acquire housing services. Of course, there is no choice but to demand the basic shelter service that is required to sustain life. The question of choice relates to how much more than the basics people will demand given their income.

The decision to acquire some housing services is realized when a person rents (or buys) a particular housing unit. In essence, this reflects a decision about "how much housing services." Housing units of comparable size naturally yield very different flows of services because of location, age, built-in amenities, etc. and they will bear rents (or prices) that reflect this difference. Each level of housing services has a cost associated with it and, in general, the higher the level of service the higher the rent (or puchase price).

Status-faction

Since most of us have a limited income, we must choose between alternative uses of that income. Aside from satisfying a basic need for shelter, housing perhaps provides recreation, possibly a claim to social standing and often a level of convenience to facilitate other activities. Even the most casual examination of current housing use would suggest that the "basic need" motivation is by far the smaller part in the determination of the effective demand for housing. This fact was noted nearly a century ago by one of the fathers of economic theory, Alfred Marshall:

> "House room satisfies the imperative need for shelter from the weather; but that need plays very little part in the effective demand for house room . . . relatively large and well-appointed house room is . . . at once a 'necessity for efficiency' and the most convenient and obvious way of advancing a material claim to social distinction."[4]

We can assume, then, that most of the characteristics of housing services are close competitors for other things in the typical family budget.[5] The need for "status" can perhaps be satisfied by buying a "fancy" car, a "fancy" boat or a "fancy" house or apartment unit depending on the person's preferences and life style. The range and variability of preferences is well illustrated by the fact that in certain circles "status-faction" flows from driving a much smaller and less expensive car than one's income could comfortably support. Recreation can flow from the facilities provided in a house or apartment, holiday trips, pub crawling, bowling nights, television, movies, etc. The choice that is made will depend on an individual's preferences, his total income, the price of housing services and the price of other things.[6]

[4]Alfred Marshall, Principles of Economics, first published in 1890, 8th Edition, MacMillan, 1920, P. 88.

[5]The colloquial expression "house poor", for example, describes an individual or family that has displaced most recreation expenditures by committing income to the purchase or maintenance of a house.

[6]The point is that the housing services expenditure-decision is inextricably bound up with other expenditure decisions and will necessarily reflect the choices that an individual makes over this range of expenditures. For example, if the difference

Summary

All of the foregoing has been "in aid of" isolating several important characteristics about the demand for housing services:

1. The demand for housing services *over and above* the minimum standard will be determined by income, the price of housing services and the prices of expenditures that compete with housing.
2. The existence of legal minimum standards reduces the choice of some consumers because the minimum standard may well be above the basic shelter requirement of some consumers.[7]
3. The need for shelter is only one of the determinants of the demand for housing — the wants for social standing, recreation and other things play an equally important role in determining demand.

between an apartment without a view and one with a view changes from 2 nights pub-crawling to 1 night or from 10 to 5 nights bowling either because pub-crawling and bowling become more expensive or because apartments with a view become cheaper, an individual may decide to move to an apartment with a view. The decision to move would be reflecting the judgement that an apartment with a view is preferred to one night's pub-crawling or five nights bowling but not preferred to two nights pub-crawling or ten nights bowling.

[7]An interesting case in point is the confrontation in 1974 between the tenants of apartments in 1601 Comox Street, Vancouver and the City of Vancouver with regard to a new city ordinance requiring the construction of two covered stairwells or a sprinkler system in the building. The building had satisfied all requirements prior to the new ordinance which was made retroactive. The tenants unanimously expressed the opinion that they did not feel that the modification was necessary and that they did not want the added cost in the form of higher rent. The city council rejected the appeal of their landlord and the tenants will be forced to occupy higher cost (higher standard?) accommodation than they would prefer. Also, since all similar accommodation is affected by the new law they cannot avoid it by moving.

II THE SUPPLY OF HOUSING SERVICES

(i) Current supply

The economics of the supply of housing is similar to the economics of capital intensive industries like smelting, refining or paper manufacturing. In order to sell housing services in a given year a landlord must make a housing unit available. Whether this involves an existing structure, the renovation of an existing structure, or the construction of a new building, it always entails a large capital investment and, hence, a high capital output ratio. (That is, the cost of a housing unit is high relative to current gross rents, which are a rough measure of "output".)

In addition to capital, the provision of housing services entails various current costs that amount to about a third of the total: the wages of labour (for maintenance, and janitorial services), materials (oil, gas, paint, etc.) and managerial and entrepreneurial talents. The supplier/landlord also incurs a property-tax cost that is related, more or less, to the amount of housing service that he produces.[8]

A fixed supply

Because the supply of housing is provided from a *fixed number* of houses or apartments at a given time there is a natural tendency to regard the supply of housing services as fixed in the short run. That this is not strictly true, however, can be inferred from the fact that roughly 38 per cent of the costs incurred in the provision of rental housing are current costs unrelated to the provision or maintenance of capital.[9] Thus it is possible for the supply of housing services to fall to some extent, even in the short run.[10] It is not as

[8]Property taxes are assessed on some appraised value that ultimately depends on rents and accordingly an increased flow of housing services leads to increased taxes.

[9]J.G. Cragg, "Rent Control Report", Page 51, Table 2. This report was commissioned by the British Columbia Rentalsman to determine what the "Allowable Rent Increase" under the province's rent control legislation ought to be. Other similar evidence on the current costs associated with the supply of housing services are to be found in L.B. Smith, *Housing in Canada,* Central Mortgage and Housing Corporation, Ottawa, 1971, Pages 16, 17.

[10]It is important to distinguish between the *supply* of housing services and the *consumption* of housing services. It is possible, for example, that a landlord's reduction in janitorial services will be offset by the tenant providing more services himself. This clearly represents a reduction (shift) in the supply of services but no fall in consumption.

obvious that the supply can be very greatly increased but some increase is possible. Lower average vacancy rates amount to increased production of services — i.e. more intensive utilization of the stock — as do increases in services and amenities and reconstruction or decoration of existing suites. The proliferation of "basement suites" in tight housing markets is a case in point.

An interesting example of the extent to which the supply of housing services can rise in the short run under the pressure of events is to be found in Professor Milton Friedman's analysis of the San Francisco earthquake of 1906. (Reprinted in this volume). During the three days that the tremors and fires lasted the city lost about half of its housing units. And, even though there was a substantial exodus of people from the city, the half of the housing stock that survived the earthquake had for many months to absorb about a fifth of the population in addition to former inhabitants. In other words, each house had to provide shelter for about 40 per cent more people than it had before the earthquake!

In general, however, aside from marginal adjustments, increases in the supply of housing services depend on increases in the basic stock of housing units. Investment in housing units in turn depends on a variety of factors, only some of which are determined in the housing market. In the next section, therefore, we identify some of the elements that appear to determine the level of housing investment.

(ii) Investment in housing units

There is a supply of housing services generated in the private sector because investment in the production of housing services yields (or did yield) an attractive rate of return. In order to isolate the principles involved we will consider the position of a landlord (or a prospective landlord) at a particular point in time.

(a) Will there be a demand for the units once they are built?
(b) What will the market rent be at the time they are ready (assuming that they can be rented at the market rent)?
(c) What will the variable costs be at the time when the units are ready?
(d) What rate of return could be realized on some other form of investment?

(e) What tax policy will apply in the calculation of net income tax payable on the income from the investment?

The basic uncertainty

The first question addresses the basic uncertainty that is associated with rental housing from the point of view of the landlord. Not only must a prospective landlord guess what future demand in general will be, but he must also attempt to forecast the demand for the particular kind of units that he is proposing to build. In order to assess the future course of demand a landlord would, in theory, have to calculate the net increase in demand resulting from the net increase in the number of households, the rise in incomes and changes in relative prices. In practice, precise information along these lines is not available. Landlords must therefore rely on their own judgements about current indicators of housing service demand.

The competitive return on investment

Having determined that a demand for the units might exist the landlord must then calculate the prospects for the rate of return on the investment. Most often this calculation is based on current costs and current rents. A critical variable in this calculation is the rate of interest that must be paid to obtain mortgage funds. If it seems likely that the provision of more housing services will yield a profit, the landlord must then compare the net after-tax return on his equity (the down payment) with the return he could get from other investments. Two special factors have influenced this comparison in the past: prospects for capital gain and tax deferments.

The change in capital value is the difference between the purchase price and the selling price of an asset. The price at which a housing unit will sell is determined by "the discounted value of the future stream of net income that it will yield".[11] That is, since a dollar today is worth more than a dollar next year, (because today's dollar would yield interest if it was invested) next year's dollar must be dis-

[11]There is apparently a rule of thumb in the housing industry that a housing unit should sell at, say, 8 times gross rents. This is equivalent to assuming that the housing unit is a perpetual bond and using a discount rate of 12.5% on gross return to calculate price.

counted (or reduced) by the interest rate. Accordingly, a general tendency for rents to rise, with no offsetting rise in interest rates, would lead to a rise in the selling price of existing units. If there has been a recent record of such gains being realized a landlord might well take this into account in calculating the prospective rate of return on his investment.

The opportunity for tax deferment arises to the extent that capital consumption allowances can be charged against total income and if the landlord has income from other sources. Thus, for example, some professional people with a large income became landlords prior to 1971, simply because the capital consumption allowances, then permitted under Federal tax law, could be used to reduce their current tax liability.[12] In 1971, the tax law was changed to prevent the use of investment in rental accommodation as a tax deferral device.

Having made the calculation of the "probable" after tax return on his capital, the landlord would then compare this return to those available on comparable investments. A possible comparison might be that between the rate of return on investment in housing and that on long-term government bonds. If that comparison is made the landlord would have to take into account the fact that housing investment involves greater risk and greater effort than investment in government bonds.

Disinvestment

All of the foregoing discussion has been couched in terms of prospective additions to the rental housing stock. It is clear, however, that the outcome of the financial arithmetic might be a decision not to invest or a decision to convert existing rental housing to other uses. Since the potential for conversion is limited, the potential for disinvestment is correspondingly limited in the short run. However, this does not imply that the supply of rental housing *services* cannot fall — as was demonstrated above.

One method of disinvestment that has become popular

[12]Upon sale of the asset, the taxes on the accumulated capital consumption were recovered by the government. Unless, of course, the proceeds were reinvested in another rental property, which postponed the recovery until that property was sold.

in Canada in recent years is the sale of apartments as condominiums. A combination of consumer acceptance and the development of legal provisions have made this possible. This innovation has had a fairly substantial impact on the economics of housing investment — particularly, on the price of urban land — about which more is said in a following section.

(iii) The dynamics of rental housing investment

One implication of the sort of investment behaviour outlined above is that the pattern of investment in any one market area is inherently cyclical. Surges in the demand for housing services produce a reduction in vacancy rates which, in turn, produce a surge in investment (assuming, of course, that rates of return and the availability of capital permit the investment to be realized). The uneven advance of incomes and family formation together with changes in patterns of migration are reflected in uneven rates of investment in different areas.

This inherent cyclical pattern is, by turns, offset and amplified by the effects of national monetary policy and other developments that change relative rates of return by altering costs and expected revenues. In particular, the costs and availability of mortgage funds could well stem an advance in housing investment that is due to an expected surge in demand for housing services.

III. SOME REMARKS ON OWNER-OCCUPIERS AS LANDLORD-TENANTS

The market for housing is formed by the interaction of supply behaviour with demand behaviour. In Canada, six out of ten dwellings are owner-occuped.[13] So in 60 per cent of the cases both the supply and the demand for housing services come from the owner-occupier who is, in effect, his own landlord.

[13] *Perspective Canada,* Statistics Canada, Information Canada, 1974, Page 214. The extent of owner-occupation ranges from 76% in the Atlantic Provinces to 51% in Quebec. Latest data is for 1971, but there is no reason to think that either the magnitudes or the relationships have changed substantially. In 1971, B.C. stood at 67%, the Prairie Provinces at 70% and Ontario at 68%.

In such cases the general model outlined above still applies, but it is necessary to modify both the demand and the supply sides of the market to account for the effects that ownership itself has.

For example, the flow of housing services yielded by a house that is owner-occupied is probably subjectively higher than that yielded by an identical house that is rented. Owner-occupiers receive what one might call a "psychic satisfaction" from home ownership (a "person's" home is "its" castle). Assuming that this is the case and that the amount of psychic satisfaction varies with the quantity of housing services, we can safely assume that owner-occupation increases the measured demand for housing services at every price. Owner-occupiers should, for this reason, be willing to pay a higher price for a given marketable quantity of housing services than tenants are willing to pay.

The owner-occupier as a supplier/consumer of housing services will also tend to behave differently with respect to measured variables than the landlord. This is due to the fact that the income from a house that is owner-occupied is not taxed. Assuming that a landlord and an owner-occupier have the same access to capital, face the same maintenance and repair expenditures, and have similar expectations of capital gain, they will receive identical before tax income from a given house (assuming that they both "rent" the house at the going rate). However, the owner-occupier pays no tax on the income from his house whereas the landlord must pay tax. Therefore, the landlord's after-tax return on his capital will always be less than that of the owner-occupier. The implication of this is that housing investment by owner-occupiers will be less sensitive to variations in the rate of return than investment by prospective landlords.

A digression on condominiums

The condominium phenomenon is a good illustration of the impact of owner-occupation. Tenants who have access to capital and high enough incomes are increasingly switching to owner-occupation of condominium apartments, where they effectively pay "rent" at a higher level than they would have if they had been tenants in the same building. They are willing to pay a higher rent because of the factors mentioned above and because currently there are prospects for a capital gain on re-sale — gain that is not subject to tax.

Quite apart from the standard attractions of owner-occupation, the federal and provincial governments have for years (and increasingly, recently) encouraged home ownership with a variety of tax advantages, special mortgage arrangements and direct grants.

The impact of the shift toward condominium ownership is most obvious in the price of urban land, which is largely determined by the value that people place on its "services". In the case of rental apartments, the price that people are willing to pay in rents to acquire an apartment in a particular location determines the price that a landlord/developer can afford to pay for land. Given that an apartment in a condominium project in exactly the same location will attract a higher "rent" (or what is the same be valued more highly by an owner-occupier) a developer who is building a condominium can afford to bid a higher price for the land than he could if he were building a rental apartment. Thus, the net impact of the condominium phenomenon has been to increase the price of urban land and in the process, to increase the rents that must prevail before apartment construction can profitably be undertaken.

IV. RENTS

The price of houses, like that of other expensive, durable commodities such as automobiles, is difficult to analyze — particularly over a period of time. In most markets the price is readily observable and relatively easy to analyze. To take an everyday example, the price of bread in 1975 is readily observable and can easily be compared with the price of bread in 1950 — the product hasn't changed.

A rent, however, is the result of multiplying a given set of housing characteristics by the price of each of these characteristics. Accordingly, a change in rents can reflect either a change in the price of some of the characteristics or a change in the composition of the set.[14]

[14]See Muth, Op. Cit.

The difficulties become obvious in comparing rents in 1950 and rents in 1975. A two-bedroom apartment in 1975 in a 10-storey apartment building with swimming pool, recreation areas, elevators, underground parking, enclosed fire escape, etc. is clearly different than a two-bedroom apartment in a 3-storey walk-up such as might have been considered good quality accommodation in 1950.[15] Therefore, it would not be appropriate to compare the rents on these two units without somehow adjusting for the change in the characteristics.

A change in rents on a given housing unit implies a change in the supply-demand conditions for the characteristics of that housing unit. That is, what we have been calling *housing services* amounts to characteristics of housing units and a rent represents some flow of services (or list of characteristics) multiplied by the price of each of these characteristics.

For example, location is a very important characteristic of housing because it influences the amount of time that people must spend travelling to and from their place of work. There is typically a high demand for "proximity" and, for this reason, apartments near the activity centre of a city usually have high rents relative to the amenities supplied. For the same reason, efficient rapid transit systems usually have the effect of reducing the price that people must pay for proximity. That is because rapid transit effectively increases the supply of apartments within, say, 20 minutes from the activity centre. Number of bedrooms, height of building and proximity to natural environments are other identifiable characteristics that have a more or less well-defined price.

As the demand for, and supply of, these characteristics rises and falls, the prices of the characteristics change and so the rents on the apartments involved change.

In terms of our supply and demand model, then, changes in the price of housing services that lie behind changes in rents perform two functions:

1. They cause tenants to reassess their demand for housing services of all kinds.

[15]In constructing its rent index Statistics Canada makes an adjustment to take this sort of development into account.

2. They alter rents on a given sort of housing unit and hence lead landlords or prospective landlords to reassess the supply of housing services that they bring on the market. (Provided that the change in rents is viewed as permanent).

V. A HOUSING SHORTAGE?

A concept that appears regularly in the debate about housing is that of a shortage. This concept is sometimes *misused* and often *confused* with the notion of scarcity. Everything is *scarce* owing, if not, as we are told, to the indiscretions of Adam and Eve, then to the nature of things. There are *shortages* of very few things.

One of the most remarkable aspects of North American society is the fact that such a large variety of products are available in exactly the right volume. Seldom is it that one hears of a long-standing shortage or surplus of commodities. Notable exceptions to this general rule are those commodities that are the subject of government regulation, are produced by government or depend upon a resource that is subject to government control.

The principal reason for this remarkable fact is that price movements, in general, are permitted to "clear the market". Just as nature will not permit a vacuum to exist, a market (which is nothing more than the interaction of people wanting to sell and people wanting to buy) will eradicate surpluses and shortages if it is permitted to do so. It does this by "signalling" to consumers and producers by means of changes in prices that they should alter their behaviour.

The notions of "surplus" and "shortage" have meaning only with respect to inappropriate prices. A surplus exists because the price is too high: a shortage exists because the price is too low.

Housing shortages produce rising rents that lead to a *decrease* in the quantity of housing services demanded and an *increase* in the quantity of housing services supplied until the shortage is eliminated. Surplus housing produces falling rents that lead to a reduction in the quantity supplied and an increase in the quantity demanded until the surplus is eliminated.[16] [17]

VI. PRICE CONTROLS

In general, since both shortages and surpluses are the result of an inappropriate price it is not surprising that artificially-maintained prices lead to either surpluses or shortages. We are all too familiar with the effects of government price maintenance programs for agricultural producers; surplus eggs, chicken and wheat have fed many newspaper stories and Parliamentary debates in the last decade. A price held above the equilibrium price (that is, the price that consumers and producers would jointly determine in the absence of controls) is bound to create a surplus. This is because it encourages consumers to demand less and producers to supply more than they would if the price were allowed to fall.

Similarly, a price that is set too low encourages consumers to buy more than they would at a higher price and producers to supply less than they would at a higher price.

[16]Take, for example, a surplus of televisions. The first indication that a surplus is developing (because of either overproduction or a fall in demand) is a buildup in dealer inventory. Dealers, finding themselves with excess stocks, do two things. First, they reduce their orders and secondly, they reduce their prices.

The reduction in price causes consumers to reassess and increase their expenditures on televisions. At the same time, the reduction in orders and the lowering of dealer margins causes a reduction in the production of televisions. Although all of this takes time, eventually the surplus is eradicated.

The *shortage* situation is a mirror image of a *surplus*. Dealer inventories fall, the dealers are forced to wait for shipments and they find that they can sell all the televisions they want at or above the "suggested retail price". Radios and other sweeteners are no longer offered to purchasers of televisions and discounts are few and far between. In other words, the effective price of televisions tends to rise.

For their part, consumers reassess their desire to purchase a television given the effective price and at least some decide that they can do without a new set. The net effect of these interactions is a reduction in the quantity of televisions demanded, and an increase in the supply until the shortage is eliminated.

[17]For an excellent discussion of the notion of a housing shortage, see the article by Professors Friedman and Stigler in this volume.

A price control is a tax

Another way to look at this is that if a price is kept low by legislation, the low price becomes, in effect, a tax on the supplier. The amount of the tax is the difference between the controlled price and the market price. The only way the supplier can avoid the tax is by not supplying the commodity or service. On the side of the consumer, the low price amounts to a transfer payment or subsidy which is equal to the difference between the market price and the control price. Furthermore, the more of the product a consumer buys, the larger is the dollar amount of the subsidy. The consumer is, thus, encouraged to buy more of the commodity or service.

Can there be any doubt that such a policy, that directly taxes suppliers and gives the proceeds to consumers, leads inevitably to a widening gap between the amount demanded and the amount supplied — i.e. a shortage?

That these are always the consequences of price controls follows from simple logic. If a price ceiling was set higher than the market would have determined, then the consumers in the market (who usually provide the political pressure for price ceilings) would certainly not have pressed for the ceiling in the first place. Alternatively, if both consumers and producers would have been willing to do business at a lower price (i.e. assuming that the market price is lower) they would simply have done so and the ceiling price would have become yet another bureaucratic curiosity.

A floor (minimum) price, on the other hand (usually championed by inefficient producers), would not be effective unless it maintained the price above the market price. Certainly if the market price were above the floor price, producers would want to sell at the market price.

In the short run price controls usually confer benefits on one side of the market or the other. Price ceilings confer benefits on consumers, while minimum prices (commonly agricultural "support" prices) confer benefits on the producer. In each case the benefit that occurs on one side of the market is at the expense of the people on the other side.

The long-term effects of legislated ceiling prices are seldom directly observable in the case of perishable commodities. This is because effective price ceilings on perishables have never lasted for any length of time. Shortages, caused by control, either create pressures for the abandonment of the control — as happened after the Second World War — or black markets develop and the control price becomes inoperative. In the particular case of rent control, the evidence on the long-term effect of control is abundant, largely because housing is durable.

The essays in Part II of this volume provide a wide range of experience with the effects that price control can have in the long-term. Accordingly, nothing about these effects need be said here, except to note that in the long-term there appears to be no benefits to either side of the market. In fact, the evidence is that the short-term gains for tenants are turned to substantial losses in the long-term.

The boomerang effect

It is possible for price controls to have, on average, an effect on prices in the short-term that is exactly opposite from that intended. Take, for example, the case where a ceiling price has been imposed on a market that does not have a homogeneous price structure — that is, a market where the same product sells for different prices in the same market area. (A situation that can arise either because people buying and selling don't know what the price of the product is elsewhere in the market, or because there are special circumstances in the relationship between the buyer and the seller.) In this case, the effect of a publicly-announced ceiling on the price will often be an immediate *rise* in the average price!

The rise in the price occurs under these circumstances because prior to the official price-fixing, some — maybe a relatively large number — of the transactions in the market were being conducted at a level below the announced price. In the cases where that was due to lack of information, the public announcement produces immediate effects. In the cases where a special relationship existed between the buyer and the seller, the seller can now say, "the government made me do it . . ."

In those instances where the price control is stated in percentage increase terms, the sting of the boomerang effect is particularly painful because, not only does the level of the average price rise, but the average at which it increases also rises as every seller adjusts to the "posted" rate of increase.[18]

The curious case of Vancouver

It would appear that something along the lines of a "boomerang" effect has occurred in Vancouver under Provincial rent control. The existence of a boomerang is suggested by a comparison of the recent and past experience of Vancouver with that of Toronto. Toronto was chosen for the comparison because it, of the large Canadian cities, is most similar to Vancouver. As it turns out, prior to 1974, both cities also experienced very similar rent inflation.

Exhibit 1 – Comparison of Rents Toronto - Vancouver

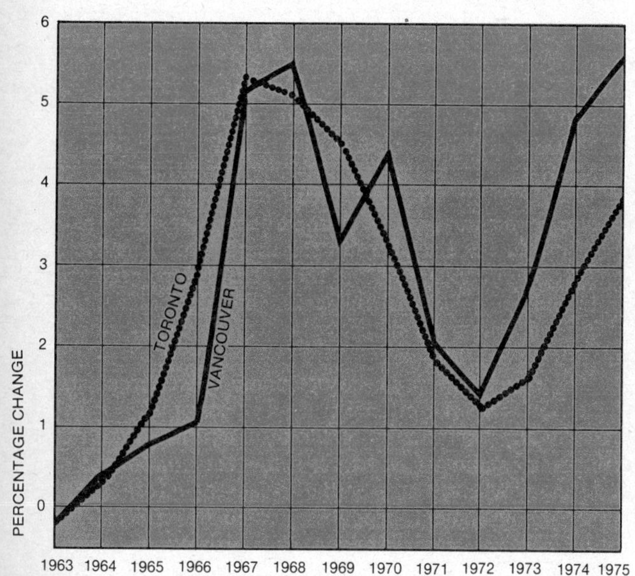

[18]Of course, in either of these cases, there may be adjustments in the behaviour of the buyers and sellers (or prospective buyers and sellers) that would result in a price below the control price. However, given the psychological impact of an "official price" buyer (or seller) resistance, that might develop in the long-term, is probably not reflected in the short-term outcome.

The rate of increase in rents, as measured by the Statistics Canada rental index (Exhibit 1), was for 1963 to 1973 about .3 per cent lower in Vancouver than it was in Toronto. On average, over the period 1961 to 1973, the increases in rents in Vancouver was *2.4* per cent, while the average increase for Toronto was *2.5* per cent. Thus, the pattern of rent inflation in the two cities was broadly similar over the period ending in 1973, with Vancouver inflating at a slightly slower rate.

In 1972, the housing markets in both cities began to tighten and the rate of rent inflation, which had been generally falling from its peak rates in 1967, 1968, stabilized and began to rise. In 1971 and 1972, the rate of increase in rents was about the same in the two cities, but in 1973, the rate of inflation in Vancouver advanced much more

Exhibit 1 — Comparison of Rents Toronto-Vancouver

	Toronto		Vancouver	
	Rental Index	**% Increase in Rents**	**Rental Index**	**% Increase in Rents**
1963	99.3	-.2	99.7	-.2
1964	99.6	.3	100.1	.4
1965	100.8	1.2	100.9	.8
1966	103.4	2.9	102.0	1.1
1967	108.9	5.3	107.3	5.2
1968	114.4	5.1	113.2	5.5
1969	119.6	4.5	116.9	3.3
1970	123.6	3.3	122.1	4.4
1971	126.0	1.9	124.6	2.0
1972	127.7	1.3	126.4	1.4
1973	129.7	1.6	129.9	2.8
1974	133.3	2.8	136.3	4.9
1975*	138.5	3.9	143.9	5.6
Average annual percentage increase 1963-1973		2.5		2.4
Average annual percentage increase 1974-1975		3.4		5.3
Increase 1963-1973		30.6		30.3
Increase 1974-1975		6.8		10.8

*Numbers for 1975 estimated on the basis of the first five months

Sources: Statistics Canada, *Prices and Price Indices,* (62-002), 1974, 1975.
Statistics Canada, *Canadian Statistical Review,* 1970.

quickly than in Toronto and the government of British Columbia instituted the first of a series of rent control measures retroactive to the end of 1973. One would have expected this to cause a deceleration in Vancouver rents relative to those in Toronto — given that both housing markets were 'tight'. As the data clearly show, precisely the opposite happened.

In 1974, rents in Vancouver inflated at a rate 75 per cent faster than rents in Toronto. The estimates for 1975 that have been made on the basis of the first five months of the year, suggest that by the end of the year rents will have increased about 11 per cent over their 1974 level in Vancouver and by only 7 per cent in Toronto.

On the basis of this information it seems at least plausible to suggest that the observed difference between Toronto and Vancouver rent inflation is due to a "boomerang" effect from the rent control legislation.[19]

[19]It is certain that Vancouverites have seen a faster rate of rent inflation under rent control than Torontonians experienced without rent control. One is, therefore, caused to wonder why Torontonians are currently pressuring the Ontario government for rent control. Caveat 'rentor'!

VII. SUMMARY — WHAT ARE THE CONCEPTS?

1. The demand for housing "services" is determined by the "wants" for social standing and recreation as well as by the need for shelter. Accordingly, family income and the price of housing relative to the price of other things have a substantial impact on the quantity of housing demanded.

2. The supply of housing "services" arises principally from the relatively fixed number of houses or apartments in existence at a particular point in time. However, new construction, renovations (basement suites etc.) and a reduction in the average time that apartments stand vacant provide substantial flexibility in the supply of services, even in the short-term. The principal determinant of the supply of housing services is the expected rate of return on investment in housing relative to the expected rate of return on comparable investments. Rents are a principal determinant of the rate of return on housing.

3. About sixty per cent of housing services in Canada are provided by owner-occupiers who are, in effect, their own landlords.

4. The price of land is principally determined by the value that consumers place on the services of the land either in the form of the rents that they are willing to pay or in the form of prices that they are willing to pay for houses or condominium apartments. Because home-owner-tenants are willing to pay a higher price for housing services than tenants, the "condominium phenomenon" has caused the price of land to rise more quickly than it would have otherwise. As a consequence, rents will have to rise if landlord-developers are to be able to compete with condominium developers for land.

5. The notions of "surplus" and "shortage" have meaning only with respect to inappropriate prices. A surplus exists because the price (or rent) is too high: a shortage

exists because the price is too low. The concept of "shortage" is sometimes confused with the notion of "scarcity". Everything is *scarce* owing, if not, as we are told, to the indiscretions of Adam and Eve, then to the nature of things. There are shortages of very few things.

6. Price control produces shortages because if the price is kept below the market price the control becomes, in effect, a tax on the supplier. The amount of the tax is the difference between the market price and the control price. The only way the supplier can avoid the tax is by not supplying the commodity or service. Since the proceeds of the tax are, in effect, given to the consumer, the consumer is encouraged to demand more. Thus, since price control taxes suppliers and gives the proceeds to consumers it leads inevitably to a widening gap between the amount demanded and the amount supplied — i.e. a shortage!

7. Sometimes a price control leads to a boomerang effect in the short run i.e. prices, on average, rise more quickly than they otherwise would have.

8. Rents in Vancouver appear to have "boomeranged" under the influence of rent control. Historically rents in Vancouver have risen slightly less than rents in Toronto. (In the period 1963-1973 Toronto rents rose 30.6 per cent whereas in Vancouver the increase was only 30.3 per cent). Since the time rent controls became effective (1974-1975) rents have risen by 59 per cent more in Vancouver than they have risen in Toronto.

PART II

Rent Control is not the Solution

Introduction

F.G. PENNANCE

McRobert Professor of Land Economy,
University of Aberdeen

THE AUTHOR

FRED PENNANCE, McRobert Professor of Land Economy, University of Aberdeen, was educated at the London School of Economics, graduating in 1950. He spent a year there in the Economic Research Division, before joining the College of Estate Management, University of Reading, where he subsequently became Head of the Economics Department. Immediately prior to his move to the University of Aberdeen in 1974, Professor Pennance was a Visiting Professor at the University of British Columbia.

With Arthur Seldon, he compiled *Everyman's Dictionary of Economics* (J.M. Dent and Sons, 1965), and has written many scholarly works on the theory and practice of urban land economics.

Introduction

F.G. PENNANCE
McRobert Professor of Land Economy,
University of Aberdeen

The essays by distinguished economists assembled in this section span five countries and 50 years of national housing policies. In such circumstances it would hardly be surprising to discern irrelevancies for modern problems or disagreement among the authors on policy issues. On the contrary, the essays are remarkable in two respects: *first,* for their topicality and relevance for current housing policy; *second,* for their broad agreement on the economic effects of rent control.

The lesson

Their common message is simple, but devastating in its criticism of policy. It is that in every country examined, the introduction and continuance of rent control/restriction/regulation has done much more harm than good in rental housing markets — let alone the economy at large — by

perpetuating shortages,
encouraging immobility,
swamping consumer preferences,
fostering dilapidation of housing stocks and eroding production incentives,
distorting land-use patterns and the allocation of scarce resources,

and all in the name of the distributive justice it has manifestly failed to achieve because at best it has been related

**An earlier version of some of the material in this essay appeared in* Verdict on Rent Control, *Institute of Economic Affairs, 1972.*

only randomly to the needs and individual income circumstances of households.

Has it been learned?

It would be comforting to think that the lessons delivered so graphically in these essays had now been learned. Superficially at least, there might appear to be some evidence for this impression. Despite considerable differences in individual approaches, all five countries appear to have been moving away from the more rigid forms of rent control in favour of more general forms of income supplementation to enable poorer families to enlarge their housing expenditure. The paradox of diametrically opposed policies — first, rent control creating additional demand and reducing available supplies; second, the use of widespread production subsidies to stimulate new building or restoration — is not so blatant as it was 30 years ago. But equally, there is plenty of evidence that the lessons have not yet been fully learned. The dilemmas of contradictory policies remain. The refusal to face squarely the fundamental issues of rent control is still piling up trouble for the future.

Canada on the brink

The topicality and relevance of the following essays has been, if anything, increased by recent events in Canada. The essays are offered in the hope that, taken in conjunction with recent British experience, they will provide a signal warning to those Canadian provinces whose feet are already tentatively placed on the slippery slopes of rent control.

University of British Columbia F.G.P.
August, 1975

1

The Repercussions of Rent Restrictions

F.A. HAYEK
Nobel Laureate 1974

1929

THE AUTHOR

FRIEDRICH AUGUST HAYEK, Dr. Jur., Dr. Sc. Pol. (Vienna), Dr. Sc. (Econ.) (London), is now Visiting Professor at the University of Salzburg, Austria. Educated at the University of Vienna, he was Director of the Austrian Institute for Economic Research, 1927-31, and Lecturer in Economics at the University of Vienna, 1929-31. From 1931 to 1950 he was Tooke Professor of Economic Science and Statistics, University of London; 1950-62 Professor of Social and Moral Science, University of Chicago; 1962-68 Professor of Economics, University of Freiburg i. Brg., West Germany.

Professor Hayek's most important publications include *Monetary Theory and the Trade Cycle* (1933), *The Pure Theory of Capital* (1941), *The Road to Serfdom* (1944), *Individualism and Economic Order* (1948), *The Counter-Revolution of Science* (1952), *The Constitution of Liberty* (1960), and a collection of his writings under the title *Studies in Philosphy, Politics and Economics* (Routledge and Kegan Paul, 1967).

In 1974 Professor Hayek was awarded the Nobel Prize in Economics.

The Repercussions* of Rent Restrictions

F.A. HAYEK

Visiting Professor of Economics, University of Salzburg

1. INTRODUCTION

The problem of rent control is still frequently judged only in terms of its impact on landlord and tenant, so that other far-reaching repercussions on the whole economic system are largely ignored or underrated. Even when some notice is taken of them, a distorted and sometimes totally false view spills over from popular misconceptions even into learned debates. It is here that some drastic re-thinking is needed.

What I shall try to do, therefore, is to deal in turn with the major consequences of statutory rent restrictions and the reduction of rents below market prices through the government financing of building construction. I shall start with their impact on the general supply of accommodation to rent and on the main types of dwellings, then go on to consider their effects on how the supply is distributed among people in search of a home, on income distribution and on the pattern of production in general, with particular reference to the supply of capital and the effect on wage levels. My terms of reference require me to concentrate entirely on the control of domestic rents, without going into the closely-related and most important question of the impact of rent

This essay was adapted with the author's permission by the Institute of Economic Affairs from a lecture delivered at Königsberg in 1930 and was originally published in Schriften des Vereins für Sozialpolitik 182, (Munich, 1930). This version was first published in Verdict on Rent Control, *I.E.A., 1972 and is reprinted with the permission of the Institute of Economic Affairs.*

It was freely translated from German and simplified by several hands, and the final result is a less elegant prose style than the author used later in writing in English.

regulation on business premises, which I have previously discussed in a similar context.[1]

If my account of the impact of rent restrictions seems exaggerated in any particular, I would emphasise that my thoughts are attuned to the Viennese scene. The ways in which these conditions differ from those in Germany are well known. The best way to dramatise this contrast is by pointing out that it will be another two years before the average Viennese rent reaches a temporary peak equivalent to 30 per cent of pre-war rents, despite there being at present no government powers to allocate or assign accommodation, in brief, no thoroughgoing state control.

Even so, I believe my principal reflections to be equally valid in a German context. Basically, deductions which can more easily be drawn from Vienna than elsewhere must also hold good where less severe forms of rent restriction are practised. The theory can be worked out by pure reason; all that Vienna provides is a convenient source of illustration. Far from exaggerating the consequences, they would be still more striking were it not for the decline in Vienna's population.

II. THE UNIQUE CHARACTERISTIC OF HOUSING

A unique feature of price control in housing compared with that in other goods and services is that war-time housing regulations have been retained and enforced ever since. The reason is not that housing is more 'necessary' than, say, food, nor that it has become harder or more costly to supply than other necessaries, but simply that, unlike almost all other consumer goods, it is a *durable* commodity which, once produced, remains available for many decades and is therefore in some ways more vulnerable to state control than, say, bacon or potatoes.

It is precisely because of this unique feature of housing that the most unwelcome of all the effects of price-pegging, its effect on supply, is neither generally felt nor even generally recognised. We are faced with the problem of

[1] F.A. Hayek, 'Das Mieterschutzproblem: Nationalökonomische Betrachtungen', *Bibliothek für Volkswirtschaft und Politik,* No. 2, Vienna, 1929. To a large extent the paper which follows is based on the earlier, more detailed study.

evaluating the significance of rent controls not merely as temporary but as permanent expedients. On a shorter view we could allow ourselves to assess their effects on the distribution and enlargement of the existing housing *stock*. Instead we must tackle the underlying problem, that of meeting *indefinitely* an emergent demand for homes at repressed rents.

Elasticities of demand and supply

We pay too little attention to the phenomenal rise in demand for homes which must occur every time rents fall below the level at which they would settle in an unfettered market. It is not merely a matter of the undoubted elasticity of demand in the housing market, reacting as it does every time lower building costs enable rents to be reduced with a corresponding rise in demand. The housing shortage which inevitably follows every statutory limitation of rent levels is directly related to the difficulty of finding new accommodation. It turns the occupation of a dwelling into a capital asset and encourages a tenant to hang on to his home even when he would surrender it at the reduced price provided he could be sure of finding another home when he wanted one.

In these circumstances a large unsatisfied demand for housing was obviously bound to emerge even without an increase in population, and the only way to bridge this gap was by the government financing of house-building. When, as in Vienna and Austria generally, there is in addition a big difference between statutory rents and rents which would prevail in the open market, the prospect of fully satisfying the demand for homes at depressed rents seems totally illusory. Despite a decline in population of one-seventh and an increase in housing stock of something like one-tenth (there are no reliable figures), no-one can pretend that the demand for housing is less than it was. That depressed rents are largely responsible for the increased demand for homes in Germany as well, and that the current housing shortage is to that extent a product of rent restriction, can also be seen from the decline in population density in almost every city in the country since the war. I shall return to the changing contemporary significance of such estimates of average population density.

Government supply in long run

Over and above this supply gap, which can be met only by government (or municipal) building schemes, we have to take into account the demands generated by population expansion, and further — and here are the basic problems of housing controls as a permanent institution — the whole range of demand created by the misallocation of the available stock of rentable accommodation. State control as an *emergency* measure could jog along contentedly enough with new building intended to supplement the housing stock built by private enterprise. In the *long term,* however, if public finance is being used to build homes the demand for which has increased due to a lowering of rents, it will ultimately have to be applied to *all* new building of houses to let. Hence — and the literature on the subject shows that this is worth emphasising — it is not enough to build publicly-financed homes in the hope that they will constitute an *additional* supply; if the aim is to keep rents *permanently* depressed, then for as long as rents are held below market rates it will be necessary to use public money to provide the *total* supply.

This development not only raises complex financial questions. Very few government authorities will want to assume responsibility in this way for all types of housing. In general, it will prove necessary to limit government building to the more modest types of dwelling, with the natural corollary that they will be the only types to enjoy rent protection. Limiting the applicability of rent regulations in this way to particular classes of dwellings, however, gives rise to other difficulties too often overlooked. For if public building operations and the supply of below-cost homes are to be confined, as they must be, to the classes of dwelling for which society is prepared to shoulder full responsibility indefinitely, they must also inevitably cater for the social class whose lot society wishes to ease, and not for the better-off. Hence it is futile to think that resources currently deemed appropriate to public expenditure on building can be used both to make up the short-fall of homes for the poorest sections of the community and *at the same time* to erect homes of better than average quality for the majority of the population. Better standards can be achieved with public funds (where there is sufficient surplus finance) to put up a number of model homes. But every attempt to depress rents even in this latter category below the levels required to pay off capital and interest will founder, unless there is available enough public money to meet the demand for all housing in this class indefinitely.

It is worth noting an unfortunate side-effect of some significance which will occur even when government finance is confined to building homes for the poorest sections, that is, those whose needs alone it can hope to satisfy. I refer to the relatively large gap that will emerge between rents for the best housing that government money can build and for the privately-constructed alternative. A large number of people will therefore inevitably settle for a home of poorer quality than they would have occupied if rents had shown a smooth progression instead of such a disproportionate variation.

III. EFFECTS ON DISTRIBUTION

So much for the ways in which rent restrictions affect the quantity and composition of available housing. How do they affect its distribution? Most experts have gone no further than to repeat and briefly illustrate the *cliché* that housing conditions are 'fossilised' by rent controls. An associated phenomenon seems to account for most of the 'far-reaching effects' I have mentioned.

The assumption of this further argument is that rent regulations will continue as at present for homes of all classes, and that the housing shortage created by rent restriction will inevitably persist. While this situation continues, the attitude to changing circumstances of anyone with a low-rental home will be governed by the conditions before rent regulation came into force. Clearly, such a distribution of available homes to rent, understandable though it may be on historical grounds, must conform less and less to diverse changing needs the longer the controls have been in force. Clearly, also, the implications of such a limitation for the mobility of manpower must be harmful.

Extent of 'fossilisation'

Before I examine these implications, however, I should first like to consider the true extent of this 'fossilisation', and where we should look for a thaw, if any. Some adjustment is made, for example, when the occupier of a controlled tenancy sub-lets or 'sells' his tenancy (in fact if not in law); in other words, when he transmits his controlled tenancy in exchange for money, and in cases — and these are in the majority — where an exchange takes place between two homes of different standards. For reasons explained, by no means all the tenants who would take smaller homes, given the chance under free market rents, will sub-let the corresponding portion of their existing dwellings or welcome an exchange. The only possible result is that a proportionately smaller share of the housing stock becomes available to those who must depend on satisfying their requirements by sub-renting, buying, or exchanging property than if they were competing freely for their share with all the other home-seekers on the open market.

Thus the interplay between supply and demand must be weighted against the tenant in those partial markets where prices are free and here too rents demanded will be higher than in an open market. The growing section of the community which neither enjoys controlled tenancies nor is catered for by government-financed building is thus worse off than if there were no protective legislation at all. In practice this means that many younger people pay a form of tribute to their elders still living in their pre-war homes; and this subsidy may amount to more than the rent they would be paying a landlord if there were no controlled tenancies.

In practice very few can avail themselves of this means of restoring mobility, and it therefore plays only a minor role. For the majority, it is a harsh and rigid fact of life that tenants cling to their dwellings, thereby preventing the adaptation of housing on offer to changing requirements in terms of size, position and standards. As a result, while there are isolated instances of population densities so divergent as to make a mockery of statistical averages, there are disproportionately more acute housing shortages where average densities are truly comparable, that is, where the number of homes on offer is comparable, than there would be in the open market.

Immobilising labour

The restrictions on the mobility of manpower caused by rent controls mean not only that available accommodation is badly used to satisfy diverse housing requirements. They also have implications for the deployment and recruitment of labour to which too little attention is paid.

In normal times regional switches in industrial manpower requirements entail considerable labour migration and, despite the unusually large changes in industry in the past decade, migrations have been blocked by rent controls. Left to itself, and given an unfettered wage structure, this immobility would prevent wages in different regions from evening themselves out, and cause marked variations between the regions.

As things stand, however, collectively-negotiated wage settlements largely rule out such variations, and two other results therefore follow. First, the wage-earner will choose to commute rather than move whenever his new place of work is within reach of his home, either on a daily or a weekly basis, even though he may find this mode of living by no means satisfactory. The wage-earner who is prevented from moving will have to spend extra time and money, which represent a cut in pay, further aggravated because regional differences have been eliminated. From the economic standpoint, this and all other expenditures incurred by people because they are 'wedded' to their homes are downright wasteful. B. Kautsky[2] points out that the cause of Vienna's increased tram traffic, which doubled between 1913 and 1928 at a time of diminishing population, can only have been this inhibited mobility. P. Vas,[3] admittedly with some exaggeration, estimates that 'the additional fares squeezed out of the Viennese public by rent control alone' amounted to at least two-thirds of the annual outlay on new building in the city.

[2]B. Kautsky, *Schriften des Vereins für Sozialpolitik*, 177 III, 1930, p. 70 *et seq.*

[3]P. Vas, *Die Wiener Wohnungszwangswirtschaft von 1917-1927*, Jena, 1928, p. 35.

Commuting or unemployment?

Commuting, however, is not always a feasible alternative to moving house, and if it is not, the result is unemployment. Joseph Schumpeter, writing in *Deutsche Volkswirt,* once gave forceful expression to the importance of the correlation between lack of mobility of labour and unemployment, an importance which cannot be rated too highly. I shall merely mention one example of it which came to my notice recently.

A manufacturer of my acquaintance with a factory in a small town some five hours from Vienna and an office in Vienna itself went to the labour exchange in Vienna to ask for an electrical fitter for his provincial factory. Twenty or so fitters, some of whom had been out of work for a long time, applied for the vacancy, but every one of them withdrew rather than give up a protected tenancy in Vienna for unprotected works accommodation. Weeks later the industrialist had still not found his fitter. Every manufacturer in Austria with a factory outside the main industrial centres can tell you countless similar stories.

I would almost go as far as to say that when the reduced rents policy succeeds in providing low-cost homes for *all-comers* the repercussions will be even more disastrous. We should not forget that city-dwellers, who form the bulk of those living in rented accommodation, are not the only ones who move. Every successful attempt to provide low-cost rented accommodation in an urban area must also accentuate the drift from the countryside to the towns. No-one would wish, whether for economic or for social reasons, artifically to encourage the growth of mammoth cities. Yet such is the inevitable consequence of inhibiting rent increases which act as a useful brake on this drift to the towns. The greatest harm must come from aiding it in boom periods, as unemployment must inevitably shoot up in any subsequent recession. In practice, even when rents have been buoyed up by a flourishing economy, this has also had its good side.

Incidentally, it is questionable, to put it no stronger, whether one should set out to make it easier for the poorer sections of the community to have children at the expense of the more prosperous, or to improve the lot of the urban population at the expense of the rural. Yet this is the inevitable outcome of a policy of federal or provincial subsidies which aid city growth and prevent the size of households from adjusting naturally to incomes.

(There is one last aspect closely connected with the wasteful distribution of available accommodation: the way it obscures genuine trends in demand both for location and quality. I deal with it below.)

Effect on income distribution

There is only one more point I should like to consider fully about the effects of rent restrictions on income distribution: their effect on wage levels. On no subject is there more muddled thinking. Intractable this problem in analysis may be, especially allowing for the indirect effects, but it is nonetheless vital to show how groundless is the popular belief that rent protection results in lower wages. It is astonishing to see even Pribram,[4] in his contribution to the earlier literature on the subject, propounding this belief as self-evident, with no attempt at substantiation.

What I have in mind are wage levels relative to other values, not increases in purchasing power for the individual wage-earner relative to the cost of housing. One can understand the lay person construing the proposition 'If I have to pay more in rent then I must be paid more in wages' as meaning that higher wages must follow in the wake of higher rents. But an economist who comes to this conclusion must suddenly have abandoned his scientific thought processes. Pribram's remarks indeed show this clearly, for he writes:

> 'since . . . after controlled rents had been *adjusted* by law to wages . . . statutory rights and not economic justice were what *determined* rents, all those commodities in whose cost wages were a component went down in price . . .'

This passage suffices to show that Pribram has decided not to analyse wage formation, on the ground that there is no need for it, and to substitute a notional 'just' wage. Indeed this is the only way his argument can be made to hang together; yet on it is based the popularly-held belief in the efficacy of rent control as a stimulus to production.

[4]Pribram, *Schriften des Vereins für Sozialpolitik,* 177, I, 1930, p. 48.

In my own mind I am clear beyond all doubt that a cost theory such as Pribram probably has in mind, even as a relatively short-term expedient tailored to fit the present circumstances, does not stand up to the evidence. If we appraise the present state of the labour market, ruled as it is by collective bargaining, our starting point is that to every wage bracket there corresponds a given number of earners. It follows that the scale of wage increases the unions can push through depends on the strength of "workers' solidarity", that is, on whether unemployment benefit is generous enough to deter those who would be priced out of their jobs from accepting work for less than the new rates. There is no need to point out that even if rents were higher industry could not employ more than a given number of work-people within a given wage bracket. Nor should it be assumed that an all-round increase in rents and other prices would substantially alter the position of the unions.

Conversely, what is certain is that to an unemployed worker a controlled tenancy is the equivalent of a substantially higher unemployment benefit. In other words, rent controls have the same effect as a rise in unemployment benefit in reducing pressure on the labour market from the unemployed. Accordingly, it can be argued more forcefully that wages are *raised* rather than restrained by rent control — and that this is more important than its effect on the supply of workers.

Admittedly this applies only if there is an all-round increase in rents and all other prices, and it is probable that, if rents were suddenly to soar, as they would do if controls were abruptly lifted, such a psychological change would come over the working population that the unions might venture to press wage claims leading to a rate of unemployment higher than would previously have been tolerated. However, this has nothing in common with the generally accepted view that rent controls help to keep production costs down.

Indirect effects on demand

Moreover, the direct effects of rent controls on the supply of manpower through their influence on wages are grossly exaggerated, in whichever direction one believes them to operate.

A far larger role is played by specific indirect effects on demand, which influence industry's ability to pay higher wages. This form of wage-pegging, which is ultimately due to rent control, is totally different from its depressant effect on wages, which has been given such prominence, and can only be regarded as harmful. The effects I have in mind are principally those which come into play in a rather roundabout way, *via* the investment of capital. They are reinforced by a host of other uneconomic practices, some already touched on and some that remain to be mentioned, such as the distortions and inefficient deployment of available productive resources which rent control brings in its wake; such practices inevitably bring down the demand price of human labour.

IV. EFFECT ON SUPPLY OF CAPITAL FOR INVESTMENT

Current housing policies affect the supply of investment capital to the economy in two ways. First, the supply of new capital is reduced because income from housing is insufficient to repay existing loans. This is of much importance to industry, since in present circumstances a good deal of this amortisation would not have been ploughed back into housing but would have become available to the rest of the economy, at least for a transitional period. Second, and more important, as a result of public building schemes immense sums were used at one time for purposes other than those best designed to increase human productivity, that is, those which would have been served in the normal course of events but for the housing policies followed.

Public building investment distorts resource allocation

The importance of the absorption of resources by public building is best shown by comparing the amount spent in Vienna alone on domestic building (at least 700 million schillings) with the market value of Austria's entire share capital as quoted on the Vienna Stock Exchange which, the Austrian Institute for Market Research has calculated, amounted to

961 million schillings in 1929. Given the subsequent 25 per cent drop in share prices, the total value cannot now be much over 700 million schillings.

Even so we are very far from having bridged the housing 'gap'. Can one doubt that, allowing for federal and provincial expenditure on domestic housing and for all the administrative expenses of operating the present policy, an outlay which exceeds the total value of Austria's industrial investment capital must have major repercussions? Even assuming that, after taxation, only part of this capital would have gone to industry, this state of affairs cannot fail to affect human productivity, and hence wage levels.

When we try to assess this deployment of capital, or indeed to assess housing policies as a whole, our attitude to one question is crucial. Anyone who believes that the economic difficulties, especially the heavy unemployment, of the post-war period can successfully be combatted by stimulating consumption, that there is no shortage of the means of consumption but that the obstacle to the fullest use of available resources is that consumers' incomes are too low, and who consequently looks to public works of every kind to tone up the economy in the long term, takes a more benign view than I do of the present outlay on housing and the tendency inherent in present-day housing policies to push up consumption at the expense of capital formation.

There is unfortunately no space for a criticism of this most dangerous of the prevalent errors of economic theory which, originating in America, is steadily gaining more ground.

Homes not provided for the right people

Quite apart from the repercussions of draining off capital from other sectors of the economy, a further question is whether the present outlay on housing succeeds in satisfying housing requirements as well under the present restrictive system as would an identical outlay under a free market system.

This brings me to the question postponed earlier, and by the same token to one of the gravest problems of present housing policies. For what we saw earlier of the uneconomic distribution of existing accommodation applies with equal force to building operations with no free market prices to guide them. My argument is in no way affected should rent restrictions not be applied to new building. It is rather that the needs of those who happen not to have any accommodation at present and who accordingly head the queue for new construction do not coincide with the needs which would come to light if existing accommodation were distributed rationally. It would make sounder sense to apportion some of the available accommodation among the homeless, and to build new homes on a completely different pattern and in different areas, that is, homes for which real demand exceeds supply.

At present we really have no idea how much housing is required, of what size, or where. So instead of building with a view to supplementing the existing range of homes, we carry on as if new home-seekers had no interest whatever in existing accommodation, and as if the housing needs of tenants in controlled dwellings were immutably fixed for all time. For example, suppose that quite fortuitously a rural or urban district has a number of young couples looking for homes; in present circumstances homes will be built even though far more people are already living there than want to do so and even though the homes required would soon become available if mobility were restored. Alternatively, homes may be built for families with children simply because there are many such families without suitable accommodation; but at the same time there may be many older couples occupying homes which no longer correspond to their needs and which would be suitable for families.

The tremendous waste entailed in such arbitrary building must call seriously in doubt the proposition, partly supported by C. Kruschwitz,[5] that rent restrictions should only be abolished when supply and demand have balanced themselves out; indeed it leads us to question the very idea that this balance can ever be achieved in such conditions. Before the war, that is, independently of restrictive legislation, Adolf Weber noted that

> 'the basic cause of housing difficulties is . . . the variance between the extreme flexibility of present-day economic relationships and the rigidity of the housing market'.[6]

[5]Carl Kruschwitz, *Schriften des Vereins für Sozialpolitik,* 177, I, 1930, p. 48.
[6]Adolf Weber, *Die Wohnungsproduktion,* Tübingen, 1914, p. 354.

Do we really stand a chance of eliminating our present housing shortage while we persist in denying even to new building the possibility of responding to changing needs?

Value of theoretical analysis

The specific object of my paper was to give a systematic picture of the repercussions of restrictive rent legislation. If this account seems to boil down to a catalogue of iniquities to be laid at the door of rent control, that is no mere coincidence, but inevitable because it stems from both a theoretical and a liberal treatment of the problem, which are one and the same. For I doubt very much whether theoretical research into the same problems carried out by someone of a different politico-economic persuasion than myself could lead to different conclusions. Therefore, if theory brings to light nothing but unfavourable conclusions, it must indicate that though the immediate benefits of rent control, for which it was introduced in the first place, are obvious to everyone, theory is needed to uncover the unintentional consequences which intervention brings in its wake.

That these unlooked-for consequences are incidentally unwelcome should surprise no one. Everyone is naturally at liberty to weigh for himself the benign against the damaging consequences of rent control. Nor is recognition of the damaging consequences in itself tantamount to opposition to rent control. What *is* necessary is to know them for what they are before venturing an opinion for or against.

However if in my concluding remarks I am to draw any lessons for future policy from our investigations, then I am bound to say that, having weighed the advantages against the drawbacks, I have come to the conclusion that the indispensable condition for an escape from our present troubles is a speedy return to an open market in housing.

V. TRANSITION TO AN OPEN MARKET

Even so, given agreement on that ultimate goal, we are still left with the question of how best to use our knowledge of present conditions to regulate the transitional perod. A conviction that an open market is *per se* the most desirable condition is of course far from an assertion that the immediate abolition of rent control as things are is the most effective method of achieving it.

Dangers of sudden lifting of controls

Indeed, precisely because rent control means so much more than that tenants pay less rent than they would do otherwise, because it means that available accommodation is distributed quite differently from the way it would be in an open market, it follows that the freeing of the market would not only bring an extra charge on the tenant but also cause changes in the pattern of distribution.

Were controls to be lifted suddenly, these changes would inevitably take place on such a scale that the market would be utterly disorganised, with all the resulting dangers. It would suddenly become apparent not only that there was a serious imbalance between supply and demand, but also that prices for a particular kind of home in particular localities had risen out of all proportion to their value. The worst of the pressure would doubtless fall on small dwellings, as the demand for them by people obliged to leave their larger homes owing to rent increases would be considerably higher than the demand from those with the means to move into the relatively cheaper larger homes thus vacated. This pressure would be aggravated by the absence of a ceiling on rents. Attempts would undoubtedly be made to push rents up to grotesque levels, and in the initial confusion they would probably succeed.‡

In my view, the remedy is not to raise rents gradually, as is generally suggested, up to the critical point, by which I mean the point which would establish prices on the open market, and thus harmonise supply and demand, which would provide freedom of movement, and which would be reached virtually instantaneously. For the transition to go through smoothly, some prior correction of existing distribution patterns is called for.

The only solution I can envisage is to try to create as large an open market as possible alongside a temporary retention of controls in specific cases. In other words, the proposal is progressively to enlarge as far as possible the existing free-market sector catering for non-controlled tenan-

‡Editor's Note: For an analysis of an actual decontrol situation that does not support this view, see the essay "Decontrol" in this volume.

cies, sub-letting and home-buying. A basis for this already exists since, as explained earlier, an ever-increasing proportion of the population no longer enjoys the benefits of rent control. What is now needed is to block the transfer of protection, so that new home-seekers start off on the right footing, thus avoiding misdirection of future demand and also putting the maximum number of existing dwellings on the free market, but without creating a new demand by the eviction of tenants.

I hope this basic outline of the subject will be found adequate. It leaves me free to indicate in 'verbal shorthand' those measures which I think offer the best hope of achieving this end.

Practical measures

Plainly the first step must be to detach tenancy protection from *property* and attach it to *persons,* by which I mean to an occupier or his *bona fide* dependents. The inheritance or transmission of a protected *tenancy* would then cease. The next stage would be to remove controls from the largest dwellings, followed by dwellings large in relation to family size, and lastly from homes previously sub-let or sub-divided, when a landlord chooses to divide up a building rather than to let it as a self-contained unit. The conversion into flats of existing large dwellings ought to be especially encouraged, although probably little encouragement would be needed to persuade landlords to let freely part of a building formerly wholly subject to rent control. The supply of homes could be speeded up by the imposition of a tax or similar levy on the rental income not only of occupied but also of unoccupied property. Another move designed to ease the tenant's position transitionally *vis-à-vis* the market in the face of legislation weighted in favour of the landlord would be to require landlords to give long notice periods, while allowing tenants to give shorter ones.

What is of supreme importance, however, is that all subsequent building operations should align their prices with the rents which emerge from these partial markets. With this in view some public aid might need to be given to building merely to stop rents in particular areas and for certain types of housing from rising above the levels to which private enterprise building could ultimately be expected to bring them.

Even so, money from whatever source should be applied only where at least a market return on investment is to be expected, and when public money is used the rents asked should be no lower than foreseeable average rents after the abolition of rent control. And if, in order to keep rents down, public money is to be used at all, the lesson we must draw is that it should be used exclusively to build the very smallest and cheapest of homes.

2

Roofs or Ceilings? The Current Housing Problem

MILTON FRIEDMAN

Paul Snowden Russell Distinguished Service Professor of Economics, University of Chicago

and GEORGE J. STIGLER

Charles R. Walgreen Distinguished Service Professor of American Institutions, University of Chicago

1946

THE AUTHORS

MILTON FRIEDMAN was born in 1912 in New York City and graduated from Rutgers before taking his MA at Chicago and PhD at Columbia. From 1935-37 he worked for the US National Resources Committee and from 1941-43 for the US Treasury. Since 1946 he has been Paul Snowden Russell Distinguished Service Professor at the University of Chicago. He has also taught at the Universities of Minnesota, Wisconsin, Columbia and California, as well as lecturing at universities throughout the world from Cambridge to Tokyo.

He is the acknowledged leader of the 'Chicago School' which specialises in the empirical testing of policy propositions derived from market analysis.

Among his best known books are *Essays in Positive Economics* (Chicago, 1953), *Studies in the Quantity Theory of Money* (edited by Friedman, Chicago, 1956), *A Theory of the Consumption Function,* (Princeton, 1957), *Capitalism and Freedom* (Chicago, 1962), and (with A. Schwartz), *A Monetary History of the United States* (Princeton, 1971).

GEORGE J. STIGLER is the Charles R. Walgreen Distinguished Service Professor of American Institutions, and Director of the Walgreen Foundation, in the Graduate School of Business at the University of Chicago. He has held these positions since 1958. Earlier Professor Stigler served on the faculties of Columbia University, Brown University, the University of Minnesota and Iowa State College. In 1948 he lectured at the London School of Economics.

A member of the Research Staff of the National Bureau of Economic Research since 1941, Professor Stigler also belongs to the American Philosophical Society, the American Economic Association (President, 1964), the Royal Economics Society and the Universities-National Bureau Committee for Economic Research.

Professor Stigler is the author of many articles on various aspects of economics, as well as of books including *The Theory of Price,* which was first published in 1946; *The Organisation of Industry* (1968); and *Essays in the History of Economics* (1965).

Roofs or Ceilings? The Current Housing Problem*

MILTON FRIEDMAN

Paul Snowden Russell Distinguished Service Professor of Economics, University of Chicago

and GEORGE J. STIGLER

Charles R. Walgreen Distinguished Service Professor of American Institutions, University of Chicago

I. THE BACKGROUND

The San Francisco earthquake of 18 April, 1906, was followed by great fires which in three days utterly destroyed 3,400 acres of buildings in the heart of the city.

Maj. Gen. Greely, commander of the Federal troops in the area, described the situation in these terms:

> 'Not a hotel of note or importance was left standing. The great apartment houses had vanished . . . Two hundred and twenty-five thousand people were . . . homeless'.

In addition, the earthquake damaged or destroyed many other homes.

Thus a city of about 400,000 lost more than half of its housing facilities in three days.

Various factors mitigated the acute shortage of housing. Many people temporarily left the city — one estimate is as high as 75,000. Temporary camps and shelters were established and at their peak, in the summer of 1906, cared for about 30,000 people. New construction proceeded rapidly.

**Reprinted with revisions from* Popular Essays on Current Problems, *Vol. I, No. 2, September 1946 (published by The Foundation for Economic Education, Inc., Irvington-on-Hudson, New York).*

However, after the disaster, it was necessary for many months for perhaps one-fifth of the city's former population to be absorbed into the remaining half of the housing facilities. In other words, each remaining house on average had to shelter 40 per cent more people.

Yet when one turns to the *San Francisco Chronicle* of 24 May, 1906 — the first available issue after the earthquake — *there is not a single mention of a housing shortage!* The classified advertisements listed 64 offers (some for more than one dwelling) of flats and houses for rent, and 19 of houses for sale, against 5 advertisements of flats or houses wanted. Then and thereafter a considerable number of all types of accommodation except hotel rooms were offered for rent.

Rationing by rents or chance?

Forty years later another housing shortage descended on San Francisco. This time the shortage was nation-wide. The situation in San Francisco was not the worst in the nation, but because of the migration westward it was worse than average. In 1940, the population of 635,000 had no shortage of housing, in the sense that only 93 per cent of the dwelling units were occupied. By 1946 the population had increased by at most a third — about 200,000. Meanwhile the number of dwelling units had increased by at least a fifth.

Therefore, the city was being asked to shelter 10 per cent more people in each dwelling-unit than before the war. One might say that the shortage in 1946 was one-quarter as acute as in 1906, when each remaining dwelling-unit had to shelter 40 per cent more people than before the earthquake.

In 1946, however, the housing shortage did not pass unnoticed by the *Chronicle* or by others. On 8 January the California state legislature was convened and the Governor listed the housing shortage as 'the most critical problem facing California'. During the first five days of the year there were altogether only four advertisements offering houses or apartments for rent, as compared with 64 in one day in May 1906, and nine advertisements offering to exchange quarters in San Francisco for quarters elsewhere. But in 1946 there were 30 advertisements per day by persons wanting to rent houses or apartments, against only five in 1906 after the great disaster. During this same period in 1946, there were about

60 advertisements per day of houses for sale, as against 19 in 1906.

In both 1906 and 1946, San Francisco was faced with the problem that now confronts the entire nation: how can a relatively fixed amount of housing be divided (that is, rationed) among people who wish much more until new construction can fill the gap? In 1906 the rationing was done by higher rents. In 1946, the use of higher rent ceilings, and the rationing is by chance and favouritism. A third possibility would be for OPA to undertake the rationing.

What are the comparative merits of these three methods?

II. THE 1906 METHOD: PRICE RATIONING

War experience has led many people to think of rationing as equivalent to OPA forms, coupons, and orders.

But this is a superficial view; everything that is not as abundant as air or sunlight must, in a sense, be rationed. That is, whenever people want more of something than can be had for the asking, whether bread, theatre tickets, blankets, or haircuts, there must be some way of determining how it shall be distributed among those who want it.

Our normal peace-time basis of rationing has been the method of the auction sale. If demand for anything increases, competition among buyers tends to raise its price. The rise in price causes buyers to use the article more sparingly, carefully, and economically, and thereby reduces consumption to the supply. At the same time, the rise in price encourages producers to expand output. Similarly, if the demand for any article decreases, the price tends to fall, expanding consumption to the supply and discouraging output.

In 1906 San Francisco used this free-market method to deal with its housing problems, with a consequent rise of rents. Yet, although rents were higher than before the earthquake, it is cruel to present-day house seekers to quote a 1906 post-disaster advertisement:

> 'Six-room house and bath, with 2 additional rooms in basement having fire-places, nicely furnished; fine piano; . . . $45'.

The advantages or rationing by higher rents are clear from our example:

1. In a free market, there is always some housing immediately available for rent — at all rent levels.

2. The bidding up of rents forces some people to economise on space. *Until there is sufficient new construction, this doubling up is the only solution.*
3. The high rents act as a strong stimulus to new construction.
4. No complex, expensive, and expansive machinery is necessary. The rationing is conducted quietly and impersonally through the price system.

The full significance of these advantages will be clearer when we have considered the alternatives.

Objections to price rationing

Against these merits, which before the war were scarcely questioned in the United States, three offsetting objections are now raised:

(a) The first objection is usually stated in this form: 'The rich will get all the housing, and the poor none'.

This objection is false: *At all times during the acute shortage in 1906 inexpensive flats and houses were available.* What is true is that, under free-market conditions, the better quarters will go to those who pay more, either because they have larger incomes or more wealth, or because they prefer better housing to, say, better automobiles.

But this fact has no more relation to the housing problem of today than to that of 1940. In fact, if inequality of income and wealth among individuals justifies rent controls now, it provided an even stronger reason for such controls in 1940. The danger, if any, that the rich would get all the housing was even greater then than now.

Each person or family is now using at least as much housing space, on the average, as before the war (below, p. 98). Furthermore, the total income of the nation is now distributed more equally among the nation's families than before the war. Therefore, *if rents were freed from legal control and left to seek their own levels, as much housing as was occupied before the war would be distributed more equally than it was then.*

That better quarters go under free-market conditions to those who have larger incomes or more wealth is, if anything, simply a reason for taking long-term measures to reduce the inequality of income and wealth. For those, like us, who would like even more equality than there is at present, not just for housing but for all products, it is surely better to attack directly existing inequalities in income and wealth at their source than to ration each of the hundreds of commodities and services that compose our standard of living. It is the height of folly to permit individuals to receive unequal money-incomes and then to take elaborate and costly measures to prevent them from using their incomes.

(b) The second objection often raised to removing rent controls is that landlords would benefit. Rents would certainly rise, except in the so-called black market; and so would the incomes of landlords. But is this an objection? Some groups will gain under any system of rationing, and it is certainly true that urban residential landlords have benefited less than almost any other large group from the war expansion.

The ultimate solution of the housing shortage must come through new construction. Much of this new construction will be for owner-occupancy. But many persons prefer to or must live in rented properties. Increase or improvement of housing for such persons depends in large part on the construction of new properties to rent. It is an odd way to encourage new rental construction (that is, becoming a landlord) by grudging enterprising builders an attractive return.

(c) The third current objection to a free market in housing is that a rise in rents means inflation, or leads to one.

But price inflation is a rise of many individual prices, and it is much simpler to attack the threat at its source, which is the increased family income and liquid resources that finance the increased spending on almost everything. Heavy taxation, governmental economies, and control of the stock of money are the fundamental weapons to fight inflation. Tinkering with millions of individual prices — the rent of house A in San Francisco, the price of steak B in Chicago, the price of suit C in New York — means dealing clumsily and ineffectively with the symptoms and results of inflation instead of its real causes.

Yet, it will be said, we are not invoking fiscal and monetary controls, and are not likely to do so, so the removal of rent ceilings *will,* in practice, incite wage and then price increases — the familiar inflationary spiral. We do not dispute that this position is tenable, but is it convincing? To answer, we must, on the one hand, appraise the costs of continued rent control, and, on the other, the probable additional contribution to inflation from a removal of rent controls. We shall discuss the costs of the present system next, and in the conclusion briefly appraise the inflationary threat of higher rents.

The present rationing of houses for sale

The absence of a ceiling on the selling price of housing means that at present homes occupied by their owners are being rationed by the 1906 method — to the highest bidder. The selling price of houses is rising as the large and increasing demand encounters the relatively fixed supply. Consequently, many a landlord is deciding that it is better to sell at the inflated market price than to rent at a fixed ceiling price.

The ceiling on rents, therefore, means that an increasing fraction of all housing is being put on the market for owner-occupation, and that rentals are becoming almost impossible to find, at least at the legal rents. In 1906, when both rents and selling prices were free to rise, the *San Francisco Chronicle* listed three 'houses for sale' for every 10 'houses or apartments for rent'. In 1946, under rent control, about 730 'houses for sale' were listed for every 10 'houses or apartments for rent'.

The free market in houses for sale therefore permits a man who has enough capital to make the down-payment on a house to solve his problem by purchase. Often this means that he must go heavily into debt, and that he puts into the down-payment what he would have preferred to spend in other ways.

Nevertheless, the man who has money will find plenty of houses — and attractive ones at that — to buy. The prices will be high — but that is the reason houses are available. He is likely to end up with less desirable housing, furnishing, and other things than he would like, or than his memories of pre-war prices had led him to hope he might get, but at least he will have a roof over his family.

The methods of rent control used in 1946, therefore, do not avoid one of the chief criticisms directed against rationing by higher rents — that the rich have an advantage in satisfying their housing needs. Indeed, the 1946 methods make this condition worse. By encouraging existing renters to use space freely and compelling many to borrow and buy who would prefer to rent, present methods make the price rise in houses-for-sale larger than it would be if there were no rent controls.

One way to avoid giving persons with capital first claim to an increasing share of housing would be to impose a ceiling on the selling price of houses. This would reduce still further the area of price rationing and correspondingly extend present rent-control methods of rationing rental property. This might be a wise move *if* the present method of rationing rented dwellings were satisfactory.

But what is the situation of the man who wishes to rent?

III. THE 1946 METHOD: RATIONING BY CHANCE AND FAVOURITISM

The prospective renter is in a position very different from that of the man who is willing to buy. If he can find accommodation, he may pay a 'reasonable', that is, pre-war rent. But unless he is willing to pay a considerable sum on the side — for 'furniture' or in some other devious manner — he is not likely to find anything to rent.

The legal ceilings on rents are the reason why there are so few places for rent. National money-income has doubled, so that most individuals and families are receiving far higher money-incomes than before the war. They are thus able to pay substantially higher rents than before the war, yet legally they need pay no more; they are therefore trying to get more and better housing.

But not all the millions of persons and families who have thus been trying to spread out since 1940 can succeed, since the supply of housing has increased only about as fast as population. Those who do succeed force others to go without housing. The attempt by the less fortunate and the newcomers to the housing market — returning service men, newly-weds, and people changing homes — to get more housing space than is available and more than they used before the war, leads to the familiar spectacle of a horde of applicants for each vacancy.

Advertisements in the *San Francisco Chronicle* again document the effect of rent ceilings. In 1906, after the earthquake, when rents were free to rise, there was one 'wanted to rent' for every 10 'houses or apartments for rent'; in 1946, there were 375 'wanted to rent' for every 10 'for rent'.

A 'veteran' looks for a house

The *New York Times* for 28 January, 1946, reported the experience of Charles Schwartzman, 'a brisk young man in his early thirties', recently released from the army. Mr. Schwartzman hunted strenuously for three months,

> 'riding around in his car looking for a place to live . . . He had covered the city and its environs from Jamaica, Queens, to Larchmont and had registered with virtually every real estate agency. He had advertised in the newspapers and he had answered advertisements. He had visited the New York City Veterans Center at 500 Park Avenue and the American Veterans Committee housing sub-committee; he had spoken to friends, he had pleaded with relatives; he had written to Governor Dewey. The results?
>
> 'An offer of a sub-standard cold-water flat. An offer of four rooms at Central Park West and 101st Street at a rental of $300 a month provided he was prepared to pay $5,000 for the furniture in the apartment. An offer of one room in an old brownstone house, repainted but not renovated, at Eighty-eighth Street off Central Park West by a young woman (who was going to Havana) at a rental of $80 a month, provided he buy the furniture for $1,300 and reimburse her for the $100 she had to pay an agent to obtain the "apartment".
>
> 'And a sub-let offer of two commodious rooms in a West Side hotel at a rental of $75 a month only to find that the hotel owner had taken the suite off the monthly rental list and placed it on the transient list with daily (and higher) rates for each of the rooms'.

Who gets the housing?

Rental property is now rationed by various forms of chance and favouritism. First priority goes to the family that rented before the housing shortage and is willing to remain in the same dwelling.

Second priority goes to two classes among recent arrivals: (i) persons willing and able to avoid or evade rent ceilings, either by some legal device or by paying a cash supplement to the OPA ceiling rent; (ii) friends or relatives of landlords or other persons in charge of renting dwellings.

Prospective tenants not in these favoured classes scramble for any remaining places. Success goes to those who are lucky, have the smallest families, can spend the most time in hunting, are most ingenious in devising schemes to find out about possible vacancies, and are the most desirable tenants.

Last priority is likely to go to the man who must work to support his family and whose wife must care for small children. He and his wife can spend little time looking for the needle in the haystack. And if he should find a place, it may well be refused him because a family with small children is a less desirable tenant than a childless family.

Socio-economic costs of present methods

Practically everyone who does not succeed in buying a house or renting a house or apartment is housed somehow. A few are housed in emergency dwellings — trailer camps, prefabricated emergency housing units, reconverted army camps. Most are housed by doubling-up with relatives or friends, a solution that has serious social disadvantages.

The location of relatives or friends willing and able to provide housing may bear little or no relation to the desired location. In order to live with his family, the husband must sacrifice mobility and take whatever position is available in the locality. If no position or only an inferior one is available there, he may have to separate himself from his family for an unpredictable period to take advantage of job opportunities elsewhere. Yet there is a great social need for mobility (especially at present). The best distribution of population after the war certainly differs from the war-time distribution, and rapid reconversion requires that men be willing and able to change their location.

The spectre of current methods of doubling-up restricts the movement not only of those who double up but also of those who do not. The man who is fortunate enough to have a house or apartment will think twice before moving to another city where he will be one of the disfavoured recent arrivals. One of the most easily predictable costs of moving is likely to be an extended separation from his family while he hunts for housing and they stay where they are or move in on relatives.

The rent ceilings also have important effects in reducing

the efficiency with which housing is now being used by those who do not double up. The incentives to economise space are much weaker than before the war, because rents are now lower relatively to average money-incomes. If it did not seem desirable to move to smaller quarters before the war, or to take in a lodger, there is no added reason to do so now, except patriotic and humanitarian impulses — or possibly the fear of relatives descending on the extra space!

Indeed, the scarcity resulting from rent ceilings imposes new impediments to the efficient use of housing: a tenant will not often abandon his overly-large apartment to begin the dreary search for more appropriate quarters. And every time a vacancy does occur the landlord is likely to give preference in renting to smaller families or the single.

The removal of rent ceilings would bring about doubling-up in an entirely different manner. In a free rental market those people would yield up space who considered the sacrifice of space repaid by the rent received. Doubling-up would be by those who had space to spare and wanted extra income, not, as now, by those who act from a sense of family duty or obligation, regardless of space available or other circumstances. Those who rented space from others would be engaging in a strictly business transaction, and would not feel that they were intruding, accumulating personal obligations, or imposing unfair or unwelcome burdens on benefactors. They would be better able to find rentals in places related to their job opportunities. Workers would regain their mobility, and owners of rental properties their incentive to take in more persons.

IV. THE METHOD OF PUBLIC RATIONING

The defects in our present method of rationing by landlords are obvious and weighty. They are to be expected under private, personal rationing, which is, of course, why OPA assumed the task of rationing meats, fats, canned goods, and sugar during the war instead of letting grocers ration them. Should OPA undertake the task of rationing housing? Those who advocate the rationing of housing by a public agency argue that this would eliminate the discrimination against new arrivals, against families with children, and in favour of families with well-placed friends.

Problems of 'political' rationing

To be fair between owners and renters, however, OPA would have to be able to tell owners that they had excessive space and must either yield up a portion or shift to smaller quarters. One's ear need not be close to the ground to know that it is utterly impracticable from a political viewpoint to order an American family owning its home either to take in a strange family (for free choice would defeat the purpose of rationing) or to move out.

Even if this basic difficulty were surmountable, how could the amount of space that a particular family deserves be determined? At what age do children of different sex require separate rooms? Do invalids need ground-floor dwellings, and who is an invalid? Do persons who work in their own homes (physicians, writers, musicians) require more space? What occupations should be favoured by handy locations, and what families by large gardens? Must a mother-in-law live with the family, or is she entitled to a separate dwelling?

How long would it take an OPA board to answer these questions and to decide what tenants or owners must 'move over' to make room for those who, in the board's opinion, should have it?

The duration of the housing shortage would also be affected. In fairness to both tenants and existing landlords, new construction would also have to be rationed and subjected to rent control. If rents on new dwellings were set considerably higher than on comparable existing dwellings, in order to stimulate new construction, one of the main objectives of rent control and rationing — equal treatment for all — would be sacrificed. On the other hand, if rents on new dwellings were kept the same as rents on existing dwellings, private construction of properties for rent would be small or non-existent.

We may conclude that rationing by a public agency is unlikely to be accepted on a thorough-going basis. Even if applied only to rented dwellings, it would raise stupendous administrative and ethical problems.

Sources and probable duration of the present shortage

The present housing shortage appears so acute, in the light

of the moderate increase in population and the real increase in housing since 1940, that most people are at a loss for a general explanation. Rather they refer to the rapid growth of some cities — but all cities have serious shortages. Or they refer to the rise in marriage and birth rates — but these numbers are rarely measured, or compared with housing facilities.

Actually, the supply of housing has about kept pace with the growth of civilian non-farm population, as the estimates based on government data show (Table 1). Certain areas will be more crowded in a physical sense than in 1940, and others less crowded, but the broad fact stands out that the number of people to be housed and the number of families have increased by about 10 per cent, and the number of dwelling-units has also increased by about 10 per cent.

Table 1 — Rise in Housing and
Non-Farm Population (USA 1940-1946)

	Non-farm		
	Occupied dwelling-units (million)	**Civilian population (million)**	**Persons per occupied dwelling-unit (No.)**
30 June, 1940	27.9	101	3.6
30 June, 1944	30.6	101	3.3
End of Demobilisation (Spring 1946)	More than 31.3	About 111	Less than 3.6

Two factors explain why the housing shortage seems so much more desperate now than in 1940, even though the amount of housing per person or family is about the same.

1. The aggregate money-income of the American public has doubled since 1940, so that the average family could afford larger and better living-quarters even if rents had risen substantially.
2. Rents have risen very little. They rose by less than 4 per cent from June 1940 to September 1945, while all other items in the cost of living rose by 33 per cent.

Thus, both the price structure and the increase in income encourage the average family to secure better living quarters than before the war. *The very success of OPA in regulating rents has therefore contributed largely to the demand for housing and hence to the shortage, for housing is cheap relatively to other things.*

Future housing problems

Rent ceilings do nothing to alleviate this shortage. Indeed, they are far more likely to perpetuate it: the implications of the rent ceilings for new construction are ominous. Rent is the only important item in the cost of living that has not risen rapidly. Unless there is a violent deflation, which no-one wants and no administration can permit, rents are out of line with all other significant prices and costs, including building costs. New construction must therefore be disappointingly small in volume *unless*

(1) an industrial revolution reduces building costs dramatically, or

(2) the government subsidises the construction industry.

The industrial revolution in building methods is devoutly to be wished. But if it comes, it will come much faster if rents are higher. If it does not come, existing construction methods will, for the most part, deliver houses only to those who can afford and wish to own their homes. Homes to rent will become harder and harder to find.

Subsidies for building, in the midst of our high money-incomes and urgent demand for housing, would be an unnecessary paradox. Now, if ever, people are able to pay for their housing. If subsidies were successful in stimulating building, rent ceilings could gradually be removed without a rise in rents. But building costs would still be high (higher than if there had been no subsidy) and so housing construction would slump to low levels and remain there for a long period. Gradually, the supply of housing would fall and the population would rise sufficiently to raise rents to remunerative levels. A subsidy thus promises a depression of unprecedented severity in residential construction; it would be irresponsible optimism to hope for a prosperous economy when this great industry was sick.

Unless, therefore, we are lucky (a revolutionary reduction in the cost of building apartments and houses), or unlucky (a violent deflation), or especially unwise (the use of subsidies), the 'housing shortage' will remain as long as rents are held down by legal controls. *As long as the shortage created by rent ceilings remains, there will be a clamour for continued rent controls.* This is perhaps the strongest indictment of ceilings on rents. They, and the accompanying shortage of dwellings to rent, perpetuate themselves, and the progeny are even less attractive than the parents.

An incomplete and largely subconscious realisation of this uncomfortable dilemma explains the frequent proposal that no rent ceilings or that more generous ceilings be imposed on new construction. This proposal involves a partial abandonment of rent ceilings. The retention of the rest can then be defended only on the ground that the present method of rationing existing housing by chance and favouritism is more equitable than rationing by higher rents, but that rationing the future supply of housing by higher rents is more equitable than rationing by present methods.

V. CONCLUSIONS

Rent ceilings, therefore, cause haphazard and arbitrary allocation of space, inefficient use of space, retardation of new construction and indefinite continuance of rent ceilings, or subsidisation of new construction and a future depression in residential building. Formal rationing by public authority would probably make matters worse.

Unless removal of rent ceilings would be a powerful new stimulus to inflation, therefore, there is no important defence for them. In practice, higher rents would have little *direct* inflationary pressure on other goods and services. The extra income received by landlords would be offset by the decrease in the funds available to tenants for the purchase of other goods and services.

The additional inflationary pressure from higher rents would arise *indirectly;* the higher rents would raise the cost of living and thereby provide an excuse for wage rises. In an era of direct governmental intervention in wage-fixing, the existence of this excuse might lead to some wage rises that would not otherwise occur and therefore to some further price rises.

How important would this indirect effect be? Immediately after the removal of ceilings, rents charged to new tenants and some existing tenants witnout leases would rise substantially. Most existing tenants would experience moderate rises, or, if protected by leases, none at all. Since dwellings enter the rental market only slowly, average rents on all dwellings would rise far less than rents charged to new tenants and the cost of living would rise even less.

As more dwellings entered the rental market, the initial rise in rents charged to new tenants would, in the absence of general inflation, be moderated, although average rents on all dwellings would continue to rise.

After a year or so, average rents might be up by as much as 30 per cent.‡ But even this would mean a rise of only about 5 per cent in the cost of living, since rents account for less than one-fifth of the cost of living. A rise of this magnitude — less than one-half of 1 per cent per month in the cost of living — is hardly likely to start a general inflation.

The problem of preventing general inflation should be attacked directly; it cannot be solved by special controls in special areas which may for a time bottle up the basic inflationary pressures but do not remove them. We do not believe, therefore, that rent ceilings are a sufficient defence against inflation to merit even a fraction of the huge social costs they entail.

No solution of the housing problem can benefit everyone; some must be hurt. The essence of the problem is that some people must be compelled or induced to use less housing than they are willing to pay for at present legal rents. Existing methods of rationing housing are forcing a small minority — primarily released veterans and migrating war workers, along with their families, friends and relatives — to bear the chief sacrifice.

Rationing by higher rents would aid this group by inducing many others to use less housing and would, therefore, have the merit of spreading the burden more evenly among the population as a whole. It would hurt more people immediately, *but less severely,* than the existing methods. This is, at one and the same time, the justification for using high rents to ration housing and the chief political obstacle to the removal of rent ceilings.

‡Editor's Note: The actual increases that followed decontrol in 1949 averaged only about 12%. See the essay "Decontrol" in this volume.

A final note to the reader; we should like to emphasise as strongly as possible that our objectives are the same as yours — *the most equitable possible distribution of the available supply of housing* and *the speediest possible resumption of new construction.* The rise in rents that would follow the removal of rent control is not a virtue in itself. We have no desire to pay higher rents, to see others forced to pay them, or to see landlords reap windfall profits. Yet we urge the removal of rent ceilings because, in our view, any other solution of the housing problem involves still worse evils.

3

No Vacancies

BERTRAND DE JOUVENEL

1948

THE AUTHOR

BERTRAND DE JOUVENEL was born in Paris in 1903. M. de Jouvenel is the descendent of a famous family which gave France noted statesmen and writers. He studied mathematics and law. After graduating he entered French politics, but later went into journalism, becoming an active reporter on international affairs. In the latter part of the Second World War he took refuge in Switzerland where he completed his great work, *Du Pouvoir,* an analysis of present-day totalitarianism. In 1947 he was appointed to the University of Manchester where he lectured on society and sovereignty. He is now president of a bureau of economic research in Paris (SEDEIS), and editor of *Analyse et Prevision.*

Among his many writings are: *The Crisis of American Capitalism,* 1933; *Problems of Socialist England,* 1946; *Du Pouvoir,* 1945, published in English, *On Power,* in 1948; *Ethics of Redistribution,* 1951; *The Political Good,* 1955; *The Art of Conjecture,* 1971.

No Vacancies*

BERTRAND DE JOUVENEL

1. A DOLLAR A MONTH

A dollar a month will pay a wage-earner's rent in Paris. Our authority for this assertion is the Communist-dominated Federation of Labour Unions, the CGT. In setting forth its demands for a minimum wage to ensure a decent living, it produced a worker's budget in which the expenditure on rent was put at 316 francs. (In this analysis, all figures will be stated in dollars at the rough valuation of 300 francs to the dollar).

Against this figure one may set the estimate of the conservative Union of Family Associations. Thinking in terms of families, this source sets the expenditure on rent, providing adequate space, at a dollar and a half for a man and wife with a child and a baby; for a family of six the expenditure on rent should go up to a little less than two dollars.

Artificially low rents

Such cheapness is amazing. In the CGT budget, rent is reckoned as equal in cost to transport to and from work. To put it another way, a month's rent for an individual worker costs little more than six packets of the cheapest cigarettes. For a large family of six it costs as much as eleven packets of cigarettes (cigarettes, now unrationed in France, cost 15 cents a packet).

*First published in the USA by the Foundation for Economic Education, Inc., Irvington-on-Hudson, N.Y., October 1948.

Even in a worker's very modest budget such an expenditure absorbs but a small part of his income, 2.7 per cent of the minimum income demanded by the CGT; as little as 1.2 per cent of the income of a six-member family as calculated by the Union of Family Associations.

Against such estimated blueprint budgets we can resort to actual declarations of wage-earners canvassed by the French statistical services. It appears from their budgets that, on average, rent makes up 1.4 per cent of wage-earners' expenditures; for white-collar workers rent goes up to 1.7 per cent of total expenditures.

In practice there are many rents lower than a dollar a month; rents of half-a-dollar are not uncommon. Nor should it be assumed that the lodgings are necessarily worse, for price and comfort, as we shall see, are unrelated.

Such low rents are not a privilege confined to wage-earners. Middle-class apartments of three or four main rooms will frequently cost from $1.50 to $2.50 per month. Rents paid by important officials or executives range from $3.50 to $8 or $10 a month. There is no close correlation between income and rent. Rent seldom rises above 4 per cent of any income; frequently it is less than 1 per cent.

It is not then surprising that Parisians spend on entertainment every month far more than they pay for three months' rent.

Here lies an apartment

This may seem a very desirable state of affairs. It has, of course, its drawbacks.

While, on the one hand, you pay no more than these quite ridiculous prices if you are lucky enough to be in possession of a flat, on the other if you are searching for lodgings you cannot find them at any price. There are no vacant lodgings, nor is anyone going to vacate lodgings which cost so little, nor can the owners expel anyone. Deaths are the only opportunity.

Young couples must live with in-laws, and the wife's major activity consists in watching out for deaths. Tottering old people out to sun themselves in public gardens will be shadowed back to their flat by an eager young wife who will strike a bargain with the janitor, the *concierge,* so as to be first warned when the demise occurs and to be first in at the death. Other apartment-chasers have an understanding with undertakers.

II. 'BOOTLEG' HOUSING

There are two ways of obtaining an apartment which death has made available. Legally, if you fulfil certain conditions which give you a priority, you may obtain from a public authority a requisition order; you will usually find that the same order for the same apartment has been given to possibly two or three other candidates. The illegal method is the surest. It is to deal with the heir, and with his complicity immediately to carry in some pieces of your furniture. As soon as you are in, you are king of the castle.

Buying one's way into an apartment will cost anything from $500 to $1,500 per room. At such prices you may also share flats which the tenants will agree to divide. As for wage-earners, they may as well give up hope of setting up house; they will have to stay with their families or live in very miserable hotels by the month.

In short, rents are very low but there are no lodgings available. Nor are any being built. And practically none have been built for the last 12 years.

There are some 84,000 buildings for habitation in Paris: 27.2 per cent of them were built before 1850, 56.9 per cent before 1880. Almost 90 per cent of the total were built before the First World War. Most of the additional new building was carried out immediately after that war; then it slackened, and by 1936 had practically stopped.

Parisian plight

Even a very lenient officialdom estimates that there are about 16,000 buildings which are in such a state of disrepair that there is nothing that can be done but to pull them down. Nor are the remainder altogether satisfactory. To go into sordid details, 82 per cent of Parisians have no bath or shower, more than half must go out of their lodgings to find a lavatory, and a fifth do not even have running water in the lodgings. Little more than one in six of existing buildings is pronounced satisfactory and in good condition by the public inspectors. Lack of repair is ruining even these.

Owners can hardly be blamed. They are not in a financial position to keep up their buildings, let alone improve them. The condition of the owners can hardly be believed. To take an example of a very common situation, here is a lady who owns three buildings containing 34 apartments, all inhabited by middle-class families. Her net loss from the apartments, after taxes and repairs, is $80 a year. Not only must her son put her up and take care of her, but he must also pay out the $80. She cannot sell; there are no buyers.

When the owner tries to milk a little net income from his property by cutting down the repairs, he runs great risks. Another person postponed repairs on his roofs; rain filtering into an apartment spoiled a couple of armchairs. He was sued for damages and condemned to pay a sum amounting to three years of the tenant's paltry rent.

The miserable condition of owners is easily explained. While rents since 1914 have at the outside multiplied 6.8 times, taxes have grown 13.2 times and the cost of repairs has increased from 120 to 150 times the 1914 price!

III. RENT CONTROL TAKES ROOT

The position is, of course, as absurd as it is disastrous. An outsider might be tempted to think that only an incredible amount of folly could have led us to this. But it is not so. We got there by easy, almost unnoticed stages, slipping down on the gentle slope of rent control. And this was not only the work of socialist regimes but of successive parliaments and governments, most of which were considered to be rather conservative.

Legacy of First World War

The story starts with the First World War. It then seemed both humane and reasonable to preserve the interests of the families while the boys were in the army or working for victory. So existing situations were frozen. It was also reasonable to avoid disturbances at the end of the war. The veterans' home-coming should not be spoiled by evictions and rent increases. Thus pre-war situations were hardened into rights. The owner lost — 'temporarily', of course — the disposition of his property, and the stipulations of law superseded agreement between the parties. This was only for a time.

But by the time the situation was reviewed in 1922, retail prices had trebled with rents still at their pre-war level. It was then plain that a return to a free market would imply huge increases, an index to them being provided by rents in the smallish free sector, which hovered around 2½ times the 1914 rents. The legislators shrank from this crisis. Wages were by then three and a half times what they had been in 1914, and the expenditure on rent in the worker's budget had shrunk from something like 16 per cent before the war to around 5 per cent. In our times habits become quickly ingrained. Instead of regarding rent as constituting normally one-sixth of one's expenditures, one took it now as being normally one-twentieth. Also, a 'right' had developed, the 'right' to dig in. Always very sedentary, the French now had struck roots in their rented lodgings.

The legislators decided to deal with this matter in a prudent, statesmanlike manner. So the tenant's right to retain possession was confirmed but the rent was raised slightly. Successive increases were granted in further laws, all hotly debated. A new owner-tenant relationship thus took shape. The owner was powerless either to evict the tenant or debate the price of rent with him, because the state took care of that. The price rose but slowly, while in the meantime the field of regulation was progressively enlarged to bring in such flats as had not been previously regulated. New buildings put up since 1915 were alone left unregulated to stimulate construction. This exception was not to endure for long.

The fear of liberty

No systematic view inspired this policy. It just grew from the fear of a sudden return to liberty which seemed ever more dangerous as prices rose. And, of course, if one had to control the price of rent, one could not allow the owner to dispossess tenants, because in that case he might so easily have made an agreement secretly with the new tenant; so rent control implied necessarily the denial of the owner's right to evict.

What then happened to rents under this regime? In

1929, with retail prices more than six times what they had been in 1914, rents had not even doubled; real rents, that is, rents in terms of buying power, were less than a third of what they had been before the war.

Law-making on rent control continued; indeed no single subject has taken up so much of the time and energy of Parliament. But the improvement in the condition of the owners, when it came, was not the work of the legislators. It was brought about by the economic crisis which lowered retail prices. Thus, by 1935, rents then being almost three times their pre-war level, retail prices were down and owners obtained almost two-thirds of their pre-war real income. Or rather they would have obtained it had not the Laval government then decided on a cut of 10 per cent in rents as one of the measures designed to bring down the cost of living and implement a policy of deflation.

When the Popular Front came to power in 1936, the process of devaluations started again, retail prices soared, and real income from buildings crumbled from year to year.

Then came the Second World War. The return to liberty which had been devised for 1943 was, of course, shelved, and all rents were frozen, including this time those of recent buildings which had till then escaped.

IV. THE BUSY LAW-MAKERS

Since the Liberation, an order in council of 1945 and two laws in 1947 have intervened, bringing up to 119 the number of laws or quasi-laws on the subject since 1918. The new laws have provided for increases jacking up rents. Apartments built before 1914 can now be rented at prices 70 per cent above the 1939 price. But while rents increased 1.7 times retail prices rose more than 14 times. In other words, the buying power of rents was set at 12 per cent of its 1939 level, already greatly depressed as we have seen. The buildings put up since 1914 were more severely treated on the assumption that the ruling rents in 1939 had been more adequate. The permissible increase over 1939 levels was set at 30 per cent, thus keeping the buying power of these rents at 9 per cent of what it was before the Second World War. It was further specified, for buildings dating back to

1914 or earlier, which comprise as we have noted nine out of ten of the total stock, that their rents should in no case be more than 6.8 times the 1914 rent. This in spite of the fact that retail prices were then 99.8 times as high as in 1914.

In short, owners of new buildings have been allowed to get in terms of real income less than a tenth of what they got before the Second World War.

Owners of old buildings, that is, nine-tenths of all buildings, have been allowed to get in terms of real income either 12 per cent of what they got in 1939 or a little less than 7 per cent of what they got in 1914 — whichever is the lesser, the law took care to specify!

The price predicament

If on the other hand a builder were now to put up flats similar to those in existence, these new apartments would have to be let for prices representing from 10 to 13 times present rent ceilings, in order to reward the costs of construction and the capital invested. According to an official source, a report of the Economic Council, a wage-earner's apartment of three small rooms and a kitchen now renting for $13 to $16 a year(!) would have to be rented for $166 to $200 a year; and a luxury apartment of 1,600 square feet floor space would have to be rented for $55 to $70 a month, compared with the current price of $14 to $17 a month. Obviously, as long as the rents of existing buildings are held down artificially far below costs, it will be psychologically impossible to find customers at prices 10 or 12 times higher, and hence construction will not be undertaken.

Such is the differential between the *legal* and the *economic* price of lodgings that even the most fervent advocates of freedom are scared at the prospect of a return to it; they shudder at the thought of a brutal return to reality. They feel that if the right to dismiss tenants were restored, and the right to bargain and contract with them, evictions could not be executed, the whole nation of tenants sitting down to nullify the decision. The thing, they say, has now gone too far, the price of rent is too far removed from the cost.

Hence the strange plans which are now being considered by the French Parliament. It is proposed to maintain a right of occupation, a right to retain one's lodgings, and it is proposed to arrive at a 'fair price-fixing'. That is, the true service value of every flat would be fixed according to floor space, the value per square metre being multiplied by a coefficient according to the amenities, situation and so forth. Thus the 'fair rent' would be ascertained. But it would not be wholly paid by the tenant. He would benefit by a special subsidy, an inflationary measure of course, as are all subsidies. Nor would the larger part of this fair rent be paid to the owner. It would be divided in slices. A slice to correspond with the cost of upkeep would be paid to the owner, not directly but to a blocked account to make sure it was spent on repairs. A much bigger slice for the reconstitution of the capital investment would not go to the owner at all, but to a National Fund for Building. Thus the dispossession of the owners would be finally sanctioned. They would be legally turned into the janitors of their own buildings, while on the basis of their dispossession a new state ownership of future buildings would rear its proud head.

Road to ruin

Possibly the French example may prove of some interest and use to our friends across the sea. It goes to show that rent control is self-perpetuating and culminates in both the physical ruin of housing and the legal dispossession of the owners. It is enough to visit the houses in Paris to reach conclusions. The havoc wrought here is not the work of the enemy but of our own measures.

4

The Economics of Rent Restriction

F.W. PAISH

Emeritus Professor of Economics
University of London

1952

THE AUTHOR

FRANK PAISH was born in January 1898. Eldest son of Sir George Paish, he was educated at Winchester College and Trinity College, Cambridge. Employed by Standard Bank of South Africa, 1921-32. Lecturer at London School of Economics, 1932-8; Reader 1938-49; Professor of Economics with special reference to Business Finance from 1949 to 1965. Deputy-Director of Programmes, Ministry of Aircraft Production, 1941-5. Author of *Insurance Funds and their Investment* (with G.L. Schwartz), 1934; *The Postwar Financial Problem and Other Essays,* 1950; *Business Finance,* 1953; *Studies in an Inflationary Economy,* 1962; *How the Economy Works, and Other Essays,* 1970.

The Economics of Rent Restriction*

F.W. PAISH
Emeritus Professor of Economics
University of London

In view of the important part rent restriction now plays in the economic systems of many countries, it is remarkable how little attention its economic aspects have attracted. Apart from the brief though admirable discussion in Mr. Roy Harrod's *Are These Hardships Necessary?* there is very little reference to the subject in recent British economic literature. It is quite understandable that politicians should have avoided the subject, for the emotions it arouses are too deep and too widespread to allow it to be discussed in public with both frankness and safety; but it is a little surprising that British economists, in the security of their studies, should have shown so little inclination to follow up the many interesting questions which the subject raises.

In the following article, after an outline of the history of rent restriction and a glance at the legal difficulties of its enforcement, I approach the subject mainly from two points of view: the inequity of its results as between individual tenants and individual landlords, and even more as between those with houses and those without; and its economic effects in discouraging the adequate maintenance of house property and in reducing the mobility of labour. I shall put forward suggestions for changes in the law which would, in my opinion, constitute a great improvement on the existing system from both points of view, however unlikely it may be that any party would find it politically expedient to adopt them.

**Reprinted by permission of the author and publishers from* Lloyds Bank Review.

I. THE HISTORY OF RENT RESTRICTION

Old control

The history of rent restriction in England begins very nearly 35 years ago, with the passage of the Increase of Rent and Mortgage Interest (War Restrictions) Act in December 1915, This Act made it generally illegal for landlords of unfurnished houses, or parts of houses let as separate dwellings, of which either the rent charged in August 1914, or the net rateable value did not exceed £35 in London or £26 elsewhere, to charge rents higher than those charged in August 1914, except in so far as improvements had been made or the rates increased. It also prohibited the calling-in of mortgages on rent-restricted property or the raising of interest rates on them. The general principles of this Act have been maintained in all subsequent legislation.

After the 1914-18 War, some concessions were made to help the landlord to meet the greatly increased cost of maintenance and repair. In 1919, increases of 10 per cent, and in 1920, of 40 per cent, were permitted in the 1914 'standard rent', provided that the premises were kept 'in a reasonable state of repair'. On the other hand, the scope of the Act was extended in 1919 to cover all houses of which neither the standard rent nor the net rateable value exceeded £70 in London and £52 elsewhere, in 1920 increased to £105 in London and £78 elsewhere. Thus, all except the largest houses were made subject to control. At the same time, the protection of the Act was extended, not only to the 'statutory tenant', but also to his widow or any relative who had been resident in his house for six months or more at the time of his death, though these in turn could not pass on their rights to yet another generation.

In 1923, after the short but violent depression which ended the post-war boom, the first steps were taken towards the withdrawal of rent control. Under the Act of that year, any house of which the landlord obtained vacant possession, or of which the sitting tenant accepted a lease of two years or more, became automatically decontrolled. When, ten years later, the results of the 1923 Act were reviewed, it was considered that, whereas the release of the larger houses had been proceeding too slowly, that of the smaller houses had been too fast. Under the Act of 1933, therefore, controlled houses were divided into three groups. Those of which both the recoverable rent (standard rent plus permitted increase) and the net rateable value were above £45 in London and £35 elsewhere were decontrolled immediately; those below these values, but with a net rateable value of £20 in London and £13 elsewhere, continued to become decontrolled as they fell vacant; and those with still lower rateable values ceased to be decontrollable. In 1938, the second of these groups was in turn sub-divided. The upper section, consisting of houses with net rateable values above £35 in London and £20 elsewhere, was decontrolled at once, while the lower section became permanently controlled.

Thus, in August 1939, all pre-1914 houses with net rateable values above £35 in London and £20 elsewhere had been excluded from control, together with a substantial though unknown number of smaller houses. The number of these decontrolled houses was estimated by the Ridley Committee in 1945 at 4.5 million. Also outside the control were some 4.5 million houses built since 1919, of which some 3 million were in private ownership and were mainly owner-occupied and 1.5 million were owned by local authorities. Thus, out of a total of about 13 million houses and flats, only about 4 million, all with net rateable values not exceeding £35 in London and £20 elsewhere and almost entirely owned by private landlords, were still subject to control. The recoverable rents of these houses were usually from 20 per cent to 30 per cent lower than the uncontrolled rents of similar houses.

New control

On 1 September, 1939, all dwelling-houses not subject to the old control and with net rateable values of not more than £100 in London and £75 elsewhere were made subject to a new control, with standard rents fixed at the rents which were being paid on the date of the Act, or, if not let on that day, at the last previous rent paid. All new houses, or those never let before, were to have as their standard rents whatever was charged at their first *bona fide* unfurnished letting. This Act is still in force, though it has been supplemented by the Furnished Houses (Rent Control) Act of

1946, which established Rent Tribunals to review rents of furnished accommodation, and by the Landlord and Tenant (Rent Control) Act of 1949, which gave to these same tribunals power to fix the rents of unfurnished houses let for the first time. The recommendation of the Ridley Committee, that rent tribunals should have the power to adjust in either direction anomalies in the existing standard rents of controlled houses, has never been adopted. No attempt has so far been made to control the prices at which houses may be sold.

II. LEGAL DIFFICULTIES AND INJUSTICES

The results of this long series of Rent Restriction Acts cannot be regarded with satisfaction from any point of view. It has long been realised that they have serious legal difficulties. Apart altogether from the question of evasion, and even after the immense case-law developed by 30 years of litigation, the legal position in any particular case is often still obscure.

What exactly is part of a house let as a separate dwelling? Just how many acres of land must go with a house to make it a farm and therefore outside the scope of the Acts? Just how much furniture is needed to constitute a furnished house? Does a man automatically convert his office into a dwelling-house by keeping a camp-bed in it, and if not, how frequently must he sleep there to bring it within the Acts? Would an owner, with an invalid wife and three young children, who wishes to obtain occupation of his own house, suffer more hardship if his request were refused than the tenant, with only one child but a bed-ridden mother-in-law, would suffer if it were granted?

These are a very small sample of the thousands of cases decided yearly in the courts. Apart from such questions, it is often a matter of great difficulty to discover what is the standard rent of any particular house, especially if it has been owner-occupied for any considerable time. If a house was last let in 1815, then the rent paid at the time of the battle of Waterloo is the standard rent today.

Tenants and landlords

If the Rent Restriction Acts are a lawyer's nightmare, they

offend at least as much against the ordinary standards of equity. Of three identical houses in the same road, one may be let at 10 shillings a week under the old control, the second at 15 under the new control, while the rent of the third, let for the first time since the war, may be 25 shillings or more. There is no guarantee that the poorest tenant rents the cheapest house, or that the poorest landlord owns the dearest one. Indeed, the landlord of the cheapest house may well be poorer than his tenant, for before 1914 small house property was a favourite medium for the investment of small savings.

Those without houses

But the inequity of the present system as between tenant and tenant, or between tenant and landlord, fades into insignificance compared with the inequity as between those who are lucky enough to have rent-restricted houses and those who have no houses at all. It is an economic truism that the fixing of maximum prices without the imposition of rationing normally results in part of the demand at the fixed price going unsatisfied. Even if the maximum rents fixed were completely consistent as between themselves this difficulty would remain. Since 1939, money earnings and most prices have approximately doubled; controlled rents (apart from increases in rates) have not risen at all. Thus, in real terms, the rents of some 8½ million out of the 13 million pre-war houses have been approximately halved. Is it to be wondered that the demand for houses to let at controlled rents is enormously in excess of the supply? Is it surprising that rent-restricted houses are used less economically than they would have been if rents had risen in proportion with other prices and incomes, and that an unsatisfied demand is squeezed out, to be concentrated on the other sectors of the market — local authorities' houses, furnished accommodation, and houses available for purchase with vacant possession?

Of the sectors not covered by the Rent Restriction Acts, rents of local authorities' pre-war houses, though frequently higher than before the war, are in general held at a level far below that necessary to equate supply and demand; while rents of their new houses, though higher than those of their older ones, even allowing for their improved amenities, are held by subsidies at a level far below current market values. Thus, a great unsatisfied demand is concentrated on the two remaining sectors, pushing prices there far above what they would have been if prices in all sectors had been allowed to find their market level. Sometimes tenants of furnished rooms (often in rent-restricted houses) will venture to bring cases of unusually high rents to the notice of the rent tribunals set up under the Furnished Houses Act, even though the tribunals cannot give security of tenure for more than a few months at a time. But such controls, even if successful, cannot provide accommodation where it does not exist; and even if they could be universally enforced, their only result would be to reduce the supply and expand the demand for furnished rooms until there remained, for those left over who were unable to provide the deposit on a purchased house, the choice only between the hospitality of relatives and the hardly warmer welcome of a public institution.

Houses for sale

There remains only one sector of the market where no attempt has yet been made to control prices — the market in houses for sale. In spite of the fact that the demand here is limited to those able to provide at least the minimum deposit, prices for houses with vacant possession, especially for the smaller houses, have been forced up to a level far above that of most other prices. It is difficult to generalise the increase in house prices since 1939, but perhaps it would not be far from the truth to say that in many parts of the country small houses are costing from three to four times, and larger houses from two to three times, what they would have cost before the war. Only for the largest houses, unsuitable for conversion into commercial premises and requiring more service to run than is within the power of most post-tax incomes to command, is the rise in prices not abnormal.

The rise in the price of small houses cannot, however, be taken as an indication of the rise in rents which would follow the withdrawal of rent restriction; for much of it is due to the concentration upon the only completely free sector of the market of the excess demand created by the artifically low rents ruling in at least two of the other sectors. The repeal of rent restriction would almost certainly be followed by a sharp drop in the prices of at least the smaller houses offered for sale with vacant possession.

III. ECONOMIC EFFECTS

Inadequate maintenance

The economic aspects of rent restriction reveal disadvantages at least comparable with those of its legal and equitable aspects. They are mainly two: the impairment of the landlords' ability and incentive to maintain premises in good condition, and the impediments which the Acts place in the way of the mobility of labour.

As regards the first of these, it is common ground that the cost of maintaining and repairing houses has risen markedly since before the war, probably more than twice everywhere, and in some areas three times or more. At these prices, many landlords are unable to pay for adequate repairs out of the controlled rents and leave themselves any income at all, while others, especially owners of older property unsuitable for owner-occupancy, find that it pays them better to collect what income they can until their property becomes actually uninhabitable than to spend money on repairs which will never yield a reasonable return on the expenditure. The probability that property will be treated in this way is increased by the tendency of the better landlords, faced with the choice between running their property at a loss and allowing it to decay, to sell it for what it will fetch to those who are less scrupulous in their methods of management. Thus, much property is being allowed to degenerate into slums, or at best maintained at a level much below that which is economically desirable and which it would have paid landlords to achieve if rents had been allowed to find their market level. For the ultimate results of this policy we have only to look across the English Channel, where inflation has gone considerably further than here and the gap between controlled rents and those which would enable property to be kept in good repair is, therefore, even wider.[1]

Reduction in mobility

The second of the economic disadvantages of rent restriction, at least in the short run, is probably even more serious than the first. Rent restriction involves what is in effect a tax on the landlord and a subsidy to the tenant. But it is a subsidy which the tenant receives only so long as he stays in his existing house. Should he leave it for any reason, he is deprived, not only of his subsidy, but also of his right to rent another house even at the full market price. If he happens to live in a council house it may be possible for him, by arrangement with the local authority, to exchange houses with someone else in the same district, or even to be allotted a new house on surrendering his old one. But if he lives in a privately-owned house, or if he wishes to move outside his district, his chance of renting another within a reasonable time is small unless he either has access to some special favour or is prepared to break the law by offering some consideration in addition to the controlled rent. Otherwise, he will have to make do with furnished lodgings until first he qualifies to be regarded as a resident and then his name has slowly climbed to the top of the local authority's housing list. It is little wonder that the much-needed increase in the mobility of labour is so difficult to achieve.

Expedients to restore mobility

If, however, a tenant inhabits a privately-owned house suitable for owner-occupancy, there are ways in which he may be able to retain at least part of the benefit of his rent subsidy after leaving his present house. So long as he remains a statutory tenant, the selling value of his present house is probably a good many hundred pounds less than it would be if the landlord were able to offer it with vacant possession. It may sometimes be possible for the tenant to obtain a share of this margin between the 'sitting-tenant' and the 'vacant-possession' values of his house, either by

[1]Illustrations of this phenomenon can be found in Bertrand de Jouvenel's essay on France's experience of rent restriction, especially in pages 108-109 Ed.

agreeing to leave in exchange for a cash payment, or by buying his house for something more than its 'sitting-tenant' value and subsequently re-selling it for its full market value with vacant possession. How much of the margin he will be able to secure for himself, and how much he will have to leave for his landlord, will depend on their relative bargaining powers; the tenant will no doubt do his best to conceal his desire to leave until the bargain has been completed. If in either of these ways he can make a substantial profit, he can use this to pay part of the purchase price of a house in the district to which he wishes to move, borrow-the remainder from a building society or other source.

Fewer houses to let

It should be noted that every time this sort of transaction occurs a house is permanently transferred from the letting market to the selling market. The same is true whenever a house falls vacant on the death of a tenant; for it will usually pay the landlord to sell it to an owner-occupier rather than re-let it at the controlled rent. Thus, despite the delay due to the right of a resident wife or relative to succeed to the tenancy for one further lifetime, it seems probable that the indefinite continuation of the present system will result in the gradual withdrawal from the letting market of all privately-owned houses suitable for owner-occupancy.

The demand for houses to let will therefore become increasingly concentrated on the new houses built by public authorities. The satisfaction of this demand, at subsidised rents, would require not only a long-continued diversion to housing of resources urgently needed in other fields but also a continually mounting annual charge on the Exchequer and local governments for subsidies. This cost, for pre-war and post-war houses, is already in the neighbourhood of £40 million a year (in addition to the subsidies on temporary houses) and is rising by something like £5 million a year.

IV. PROPOSALS FOR REFORM

Repeal of Acts

While, however, it is easy enough to see the defects, legal, social and economic, of the system of rent restriction into which the country has been allowed to drift, it is much less easy to suggest an acceptable remedy. The mere repeal of the existing Acts, though a solution of the economic difficulties and in the long run likely to prove highly beneficial to the country as a whole, would in the short run frustrate many justifiable expectations, and bring about a sudden redistribution of incomes which the electorate would certainly not desire nor the individuals affected in many cases deserve. While some of the landlords who would benefit from repeal have no doubt suffered unjustly as compared with receivers of income from other types of property, there are others, such as recent purchasers of rent-restricted property at the 'sitting-tenant' price, who would make large windfall profits; and on the other side, while many tenants could no doubt afford to pay higher rents without real difficulty, others, especially those with children or living on small pensions, would suffer the most serious hardship. Simple repeal would therefore give rise to so many hard cases and obvious injustices that it would offend against the principles of equity almost as much as do the existing Acts, and against the public sense of equity probably far more.

Other proposals

Various suggestions have been made which, while maintaining the Rent Restriction Acts in force, would mitigate some part of their ill-effects. The Ridley Committee Report of 1945[2] among recommendations for minor improvements in the working of the system, made three suggestions on points of substance. The first of these was that the various Acts should be consolidated and their legal anomalies cleared up; the second was that rent tribunals should be set up to overhaul the whole system of standard rents and remove their inconsistencies with each other; and the third was that after three years a committee should be appointed to report on the cost of house repairs, with a view to a possible increase in the level of permitted rents. None of these recommendations touches the central problems, and, apart from the power given to rent tribunals to review post-1939 rentals, none has been acted upon.

[2]*The Rent Restriction Acts*, Cmd. 6621, HMSO, 1944-45

The recommendations of a report published in November 1949 by PEP[3] come rather nearer to dealing with the real difficulties. The report looks, not too hopefully, to the Local Government Act of 1948, with its programme for re-assessing rateable values on a consistent basis throughout the country by 1953, to provide a means of carrying out the Ridley Committee's recommendation for the elimination of inconsistencies between restricted rents; and it urges some relief to landlords, by means of increased rents and/or special tax allowances, to provide the means of carrying out repairs. This last recommendation would do something to prevent large stretches of low-rented premises from degenerating into slums, while the first would help to remove the inequity as between one tenant of a controlled house and another. But neither would do anything towards solving the problem either of the inequity between those with houses and those without or of the immobility of labour.

Various suggestions have been made to deal with the problem of immobility. It might, for instance, be possible to make people more mobile by giving to anyone who surrendered the tenancy of a house priority for a new tenancy, whether in his own district or elsewhere. Such a measure, however, would encounter insuperable political difficulties; for to give a newcomer in a district priority over existing inhabitants, some of whom had waited perhaps for years, would reveal far too plainly the injustice of the present system towards those who are not lucky enough to have a house. No solution which does not make a serious attempt to deal with this injustice either has or ought to have any chance of acceptance.

Mr. Harrod's plan

A similar objection can be made to the otherwise most valuable suggestions made by Mr. Roy Harrod in his book *Are These Hardships Necessary?*[4] Mr. Harrod suggests that the Acts should be repealed and rents be allowed to rise to their full market level, but that for a period of 10 years the landlord should be taxed the whole of the increase and the proceeds handed back to the tenant, who would receive them whether he stayed in that house or not. At the end of

[3] *Rent Control Policy*, Broadsheet No. 305.

[4] Rupert Hart-Davis, London, 1947.

the 10 years,

> 'some readjustment of wages or taxes could be made, so as to avoid any transfer of income from the poor to the rich that the abolition of the old system might entail'.

This scheme would clearly have great advantages over the present system. So long as the tenant stayed in his existing house, his extra rent would be exactly equalled by his extra income, and he would be neither better nor worse off than before. But he would now have the choice between spending the whole of his new allowance on the increased rent and moving to a cheaper house, thus freeing part of his new allowance for spending on other things. Further, since rents of other houses would be at their full market level, he would be able to find another house at a rent, no doubt higher than its previous controlled level, but lower than the new rent of his existing house. The tenants most likely to move in this way would probably be elderly people, who are at present both enabled by the low rents they are paying and compelled by the difficulty of finding other accommodation to stay on in a house too large for them now that their children have grown up and left home; but, no doubt, there are many other people who would find that they preferred to spend some part of their increased money incomes in other ways and would move to smaller and cheaper premises. Thus, the demand for house-room, now artificially stimulated by the reduction in real rents, would fall to a normal market level, and the unfortunates who compose the surplus demand, now squeezed out of the market, would be able to get a house. No existing tenant would be worse off if he stayed, and since any move he made would be voluntary, he would move only if he thought that he was thereby making himself better off.

Disadvantages

While Mr. Harrod's scheme would do much to remedy the disadvantages of the present system, and would largely solve the problem of mobility, it has three serious deficiencies. First, it does nothing, for at least 10 years, to make the landlord better able to provide for the increased cost of repairs; for the heavy tax would be just as efficient a promoter of slums as the present restriction on rents.

Secondly, it perpetuates the random distribution of the subsidy between tenants, regardless of their means, so that a tenant with a larger income or smaller responsibilities might well receive a larger grant than one poorer or more burdened.

Most serious of all is the difficulty that, while the injustice to the man without a house would in fact be somewhat reduced by making it possible for him to get one at the full market rent, Mr. Harrod's scheme would make the remaining inequity explicit and therefore less acceptable to public opinion than the even greater inequity implicit in the existing system. We have only to think of the feelings of a man who is on the point of getting a house, for which perhaps he has been waiting for years, at a controlled or subsidised rent, and who suddenly learns that its rent has risen by 50 or 100 per cent. He will receive no compensation for the rise in rent of a house he has never inhabited, while his next-door neighbour, who got his house perhaps a month ago, will receive an allowance which is not only sufficient to cover the rise in his present rent but which he will retain in full if he moves into a cheaper house. The resentment against treatment so obviously unfair would certainly prevent Mr. Harrod's scheme from being put into force as it stands.

V. A SUGGESTED SCHEME

Any scheme, to be logically defensible, must endeavour to deal with the difficulties which Mr. Harrod's scheme ignores, as well as with those which it resolves. Landlords must be given a sufficient share of the increases in rent to enable them to maintain their premises in repair, and the benefits of the amounts collected in tax must be shared, not only by existing tenants, but also by those who are without permanent accommodation.

Equitable distribution of tax

To meet these points would involve two substantial departures from Mr. Harrod's scheme. In the first place, the landlord, instead of passing on the whole of the additional tax collected would be allowed to retain, say, 25 per cent of the addition as provision for repairs, provided the premises were kept in a condition satisfactory to the local authorities.

The second difference would be that, instead of using the proceeds of the tax to subsidise only existing tenants, the Treasury would use part of it to supplement incomes in accordance with need, by increasing children's allowances, old-age and other pensions, and so forth, and the remainder to reduce the general level of taxation. They would thus increase all net incomes, but especially those of people least able to pay the increased rents. It might very well happen that the incomes of people with large families would be increased by more than the increase in the rents of their existing houses, so that they would be able to afford to move into the larger houses vacated by people without families now finding it advantageous to move into smaller ones.

Owner-occupiers

There is one further measure that would be needed to make this suggested scheme complete. Since all members of the population would benefit, in greater or less degree, from the increased allowances and reduced taxation, to impose the landlords' tax only on the owners of rented houses would mean subsidising owner-occupiers at the expense of tenants. Owner-occupiers would, therefore, also have to be made liable for landlords' tax on their own houses to provide the means of financing the benefits which they, as a class, would receive from higher allowances and lower taxes.

One of the major practical difficulties of the scheme would be to assess the tax on owner-occupiers in such a way that it would be both fair as between different owner-occupiers and would yield an amount sufficient to finance the benefits which they collectively would enjoy. This task of assessment would be considerably eased after 1953, on the completion of the re-assessment, on a more consistent basis, of rateable values throughout the country.

Financing the scheme

The amount of revenue the Treasury might expect to receive from the landlords' tax cannot be estimated with any degree of accuracy. It is, however, possible to make a guess at the order of magnitude involved. If rents of controlled houses were allowed to rise to levels which effectively equated supply and demand, the average increase per privately-owned house let at controlled rents would hardly be less than 10s. per week. On 8½ million houses this would yield about £220 million a year, of which £55 million would remain with the landlord and £165 million be passed on to the Treasury. If owner-occupiers paid a corresponding tax at the same average rate of 7s. 6d. a week, this, on 3 million houses, would yield a further £60 million a year.

The saving on subsidies on local authorities' houses would also be substantial. It is true that, even at full market rates, post-war temporary houses would have to be let at rents which would not cover more than a fraction of their present subsidies, which (on the basis of a 10-year life) amount to some £21 million a year on 157,000 houses, or about £2 10s. per house per week. The same might well be true, to a smaller degree, for the post-war permanent houses built by local authorities, on which the present subsidies are about £23 million on less than 700,000 houses, or about 13s. per house per week. On the other hand, the raising to the full market level of rents on the nearly 1½ million pre-war council houses would certainly yield more than the present subsidies of £17 million, or about 4s. 9d. per house per week. Further, the local authorities would save the whole of the increase in rents and not merely 75 per cent of it.

While, therefore, the rents of local authorities' houses, which are now on the whole higher than those of privately-owned houses, would rise less if they were let at full market price, the net gain to the authorities might be of about the same magnitude, or about 7s. 6d. per house per week, except perhaps where the class of tenants permitted to occupy certain houses was narrowly restricted, as in some slum-clearance schemes. On the 2¼ million of local authorities' houses, this saving on subsidies would yield about £45 million a year out of the present £61 million. How this saving was shared between central and local governments would not be of great importance, for the only question would be whether the benefit was passed back to the public in reduc rates or reduced taxes. If, however, we assume that local authorities retained sufficient to free them alto of their share of the subsidies — perhaps £20 million — this might leave something like £25 million a year as the gain to central government. Thus, the total yield to central government from landlords' tax and subsidy savings might be something like £250 million a year. If it were considered expedient to continue to build local authorities' houses in the present quantities at costs which could not be covered by full market rents, the remaining cost of subsidies, estimated at about £16 million a year, would begin to rise again, but only at the rate of some £2 million a year as compared with the present rate of increase of about £5 million a year.

Advantages

The proposals put forward here seem on the whole to conform fairly well to the three criteria enunciated above — administrative convenience, equity as between persons and classes, and economic desirability. To calculate the tax payable on a rented house only two factors would need to be known — the rent paid on the date on which the new regulations came into force and the rent paid in the current year. The whole of the elaborate legal framework of the existing Rent Restriction Acts would fall away.

Tax on owner-occupied houses would presumably have to be based on rateable values. Until the results of the new valuations under the Local Government Act, 1948, were available, this would lead to some inequities as between one owner-occupier and another, but these would presumably be temporary. Landlords would continue to be treated more harshly than owners of other types of property, though less harshly than at present. In due course, the tax would no doubt come to be regarded as most unjust and high in order of priority for reduction whenever the budgetary situation permitted. Pressure for its reduction would be all the more effective because the tax would also be paid by owner-occupiers, though these, unlike the landlords, would as a class be receiving commensurate benefits in other ways. For existing tenants as a whole the aggregate cost of increased rents would be larger than the aggregate benefits received, both as a result of the deduction to meet the increased cost of repairs and because the remaining benefits would have to be shared with those without houses; but the benefits would be distributed in such a way as to prevent cases of serious hardship, while some, especially those with large families, might be better off. Those without houses would receive a double relief of the injustice they are now suffering: they would be able to find houses to let, and their increased allowances and lower taxes would give them help towards paying the full market rents.

The economic advantages of the change would include not only the restoration of mobility but also an increase in the supply of the sizes of houses and flats most in demand. As people in houses too large for them tried to economise by moving into smaller premises, rents of the larger houses would fall relatively to those of the smaller ones. This would not only make it easier for people with large families to occupy the larger premises, but would make it more profitable to convert the larger houses, with relatively lower rents and therefore relatively lower landlords' taxes, into maisonnettes or flats for small families. Thus, the number of dwellings available for letting would be increased at a fraction of the cost of building new houses. The tax on such converted premises would continue to be paid at the rate appropriate to the whole house before conversion.

It must be emphasised that this scheme, if adopted at all, should be adopted as a whole. The omission of any part of it would destroy its balance, so that the introduction of the remainder might well serve merely to import new injustices in place of the old.

Difficulties

Whether such a scheme, however logically satisfactory, would ever be acceptable to the electorate of this country, or whether, even if accepted, it would meet with sufficient co-operation from tenants and landlords to render it workable, is open to considerable doubt. A large number, perhaps a majority, of tenants would be called upon to surrender in favour of other groups in the community some part of the rent subsidy they now in effect enjoy, and it may well be that the habit of regarding money rents as fixed, whatever the fall in the purchasing power of money, is too ingrained to be altered by a change in the law, however desirable in the interests of the community as a whole.

It is not unlikely that, even if such a measure could be passed into law, many landlords would be deterred by fears of trouble from raising their rents, at any rate to existing tenants. In this case, the Treasury would receive less revenue and would be able to pass on smaller benefits to taxpayers. Thus, tenants paying full market rents would receive less than appropriate compensation, especially as the failure of some rents to rise would raise the market rents of the remainder; owner-occupiers would suffer a similar injustice. Mobility would also be less than fully restored, for those with complaisant landlords would be reluctant to move. No doubt in course of time rents would gradually become adjusted to their new level, but the injustice suffered in the meantime might well discredit the whole scheme.

To meet this danger it might be necessary to compel landlords to raise their rents by assessing them on the basis of estimated market rents, but this would be an undesirable complication.

VI. POSSIBLE SOLUTIONS

If the abolition of rent restriction could be made to coincide with a general reduction in taxation its path could be made much easier. An additional £100 million or so would enable allowances to landlords for repairs and to those without houses to be given without reducing allowances to existing tenants as a class below the level required to meet the whole of their increases in rent. In this case it might be expedient to return to an adaptation of Mr. Harrod's scheme. It is true that this would perpetuate the inevitably inequitable distribution of the rent subsidies now received by tenants. It is also true that difficulties would arise in fixing the rent grants given to persons without houses; for if the grant were to be determined by the increase over the standard rent of the first house subsequently occupied, it would create a fictitiously expanded demand for the houses with the largest increases, which would drive their rents still higher. After a decent interval the new tenant could move to cheaper premises, taking his inflated grant with him, and leave the house free for the temporary occupation of a similar tenant. Allowances to those without houses would therefore have to be determined on some other basis, either in relation to need or on some kind of flat rate. Nevertheless, in spite of these objections, such a scheme would represent so great an improvement on the present system that if its chances of acceptance were better than those of a theoretically more perfect scheme it would be foolish to let them slip.

If neither of the schemes suggested is regarded as politically practicable, the simplest alternative would be to return to the methods of the Act of 1923. These would include some immediate increase in rent for landlords who kept their premises in adequate repair and the release from control of any premises which fell vacant. As a statutory tenancy can be inherited only once, it then should not take more than two generations to rid ourselves of the disastrous incubus of the Rent Restriction Acts.

5

Recent British Experience
A Postscript from 1975

F.G. PENNANCE

McRobert Professor of Land Economy,
University of Aberdeen

THE AUTHOR

FRED PENNANCE, McRobert Professor of Land Economy, University of Aberdeen, was educated at the London School of Economics, graduating in 1950. He spent a year there in the Economic Research Division, before joining the College of Estate Management, University of Reading, where he subsequently became Head of the Economics Department. Immediately prior to his move to the University of Aberdeen in 1974, Professor Pennance was a Visiting Professor at the University of British Columbia.

With Arthur Seldon, he compiled *Everyman's Dictionary of Economics* (J.M. Dent and Sons, 1965), and has written many scholarly works on the theory and practice of urban land economics.

Recent British Experience A Postscript from 1975*

F.G. PENNANCE

McRobert Professor of Land Economy, University of Aberdeen

The purpose of this essay is to provide an up-to-date perspective on the state of British rent control legislation. The earlier history of British rent restriction is set out in Professor Paish's essay.

Post-war de-control — and re-control

The main change during the 1950's was the Rent Act of 1957[1] which freed the more expensive properties from control. This experiment in de-control "from the top" was not repeated. Instead the Rent Act of 1965[1] effectively reversed the process. Practically all tenancies of uncontrolled dwellings with a rateable value of 400 pounds or less (in London) or 200 pounds (elsewhere) were given security of tenure similar to that afforded by the old rent control system. The 1965 system introduced a new concept — rent regulation — under which machinery was established for fixing "fair rents" for regulated dwellings. Application for a "fair" rent to be determined and registered could be made by a landlord, tenant, or both to the local Rent Officer or, on appeal from his decision, to Rent Assessment Committees. Until such a "fair" rent had been registered for a dwelling, its rent was effectively pegged at the level obtaining when the Act came into force. A registered "fair" rent might raise, lower or simply confirm the rent formerly payable; but once

[1]Now consolidated, for England and Wales, in the Rent Act 1968.

An earlier version of some of the material in this essay appeared in Verdict on Rent Control, *Institute of Economic Affairs, 1972.*

fixed it held for three years unless either a new "fair" rent was applied for jointly by both landlord and tenant or a change in circumstances occurred.

The Housing Finance Act, July 1972 sought to extend this sytem by converting both (private) rent-controlled tenancies and local government council tenancies into regulated tenancies at fair rents.[2] Virtually all rented property was thus placed under the umbrella of rent regulation. The parallel changes in the 1972 Act were a rent allowance payable to private tenants in need (to be financed, initially at least, by the Government) and rent rebates for council tenants in need. Housing subsidies to local authorities, formerly used largely to reduce council rents indiscriminately, were reformed to support the grant of rent rebates according to need and to stimulate slum clearance.

The explanatory White Paper accompanying the Housing Finance Bill[3] recognized the failings of rent control in promoting disrepair and reduction of the available stock of rentable dwellings by accelerated obsolescence and the transfer of homes to the more lucrative sale market. It agreed that:

> 'rent legislation cannot cure a housing shortage. It can only mitigate the effects of the shortage by giving comfort to sitting tenants at the expense of prospective tenants'.[4]

Yet it evidently saw no dissonance between these observations and the statement that:

> 'so long as there is a shortage of dwellings to let, tenants will need to be protected by rent restriction and given security of tenure'.[4]

It saw the 'fair rent' system as the lifting mechanism designed to remove the logical *impasse.* This belief was based on the 1971 Report of the Francis Committee established in 1969 to examine rent regulation, which had offered 'the general view that the system is working well'.[5] The rent

[2]The Rent Act, 1968 and the Housing Act, 1969 contained provisions for a form of 'creeping decontrol' by transfer of tenancies from control to regulation on change of tenancy, improvement of the property to minimum standards, death of two successive statutory tenants, or by ministerial order.

[3]Fair Deal for Housing, Cmnd. 4728, HMSO, July 1971.

[4]Ibid., p. 6.

[5]Report of the Committee on the Rent Acts, Cmnd. 4609, HMSO, 1971, p. 8.

allowance system would mitigate hardship to needy tenants arising from higher rents.

'Fair' rent for Buckingham Palace?

The implication was clearly that the fair rent system, if generalized, was capable of producing investment returns to landlords sufficient to maintain and encourage expansion of the stock of private rentable homes. But no evidence was produced to support this article of faith. Certainly the 'general view that it was working well' cannot count as evidence. It is no surprise to find that it 'works'. Rent Officers are no doubt sensible, hard-working and conscientious. They have a National Association, write papers, hold conferences: in short, they behave much like other responsible public officers required to produce valuations according to statutory rules. They would probably have no difficulty at all in fixing a 'fair' rent for Buckingham Palace if need be. But this proves nothing except that operational rules can be invented for any situation as long as the operators are under no compulsion to consider the economic facts of life or the effects of their decision.

Confusing the causes

The Report of the Francis Committee was painstaking and thorough; with its appendices it runs to over 500 pages; yet only four of them are devoted to the effect of rent regulation on the availability of homes for renting! Even then, the views expressed were elliptic, to put it mildly:

> ". . . there can be little doubt that the broad picture is a gloomy one. The supply of private unfurnished accommodation for renting is continuing to diminish. It would be wrong to attribute this solely or even mainly to rent regulation. The trend was there before the Rent Act 1965 did anything to halt it. The inference seems to be that this trend is largely due to the advantages of, and the widespread desire for, owner-occupation".[6]

It is of course true that continuing inflation, rising money (and real) incomes, and the substantial tax advantages

[6]Ibid., p. 82.

to mortgagor homeowners would be likely to produce a marked shift to home-ownership from rented homes. But this is a far cry from concluding that rent regulation can be whitewashed. It was responsible for the continuing shrinkage in rentable accommodation. The Francis Committee concluded its four-page review of this crucial issue with a significant table comparing vacancies advertised in the *London Weekly Advertiser* during March 1963 and March 1970. Unfurnished vacancies numbered 767 in 1963 and 66 in 1970. Furnished vacancies increased from 855 to 1,290. Since at that time furnished homes represented virtually the only free sector of the rental market, there were obviously forces at work other than an autonomous shift in consumer preferences towards owner-occupation. It is strange that the Francis Committee forebore to draw the obvious conclusion — that rent regulation had affected supply.

The economic fallacy — and economic incest

A 'fair rent', as defined by the statutory rules for determining it, is in effect what the market rent would be if supply and demand for homes in an area were broadly in balance, and taking into account age, character, quality and location. It thus specifically excludes from the reckoning the one economic factor likely to produce any easing of a situation of shortage. A 'fair' rent is therefore by definition a *restricted* rent, except in the peculiar circumstances where it is presumably unnecessary to bother with a fair rent! Unfortunately, there is also an inevitable tendency for 'fair' rents to be determined by the 'fair' rents already established for comparable properties in the area. This form of economic incest is common to most forms of valuation based on statutory rules. What it means in effect is that situations of shortage are not only perpetuated but also likely to be exacerbated unless further compensatory 'rules' are established.

In these circumstances there is little comfort to be drawn from the observed result that many applications to Rent Officers have produced increases in rent. What matters for investment incentives is the return achieved: not whether rent has been increased but by *how much.* A reduction in a rate of slide downhill does nothing much for morale if everyone else is climbing.

Control continues to creep

The Rent Act 1974 hastily introduced by the Labour government in taking over from the Conservatives, began the process of dismantling the 1972 Act which Labour's election manifesto had promised. It halted even the weak moves to rationalize council rents which the 1972 Act had implemented and with impeccable logic, extended the range of private rental regulation to include (effectively for the first time ever) furnished accommodation.

The results have been predictable and swift. Tenants occupying furnished accommodation have gained by obtaining greater security of tenure but at the expense of a significant erosion in existing and an almost total freeze-up of new supplies of furnished accommodation on the market. The recent correspondence columns of newspapers in Britain have been thick with recrimination and counter-recrimination on this score.

The overall picture has been further complicated by the one-year total freeze on all rents imposed as an anti-(?) inflationary measure in March 1974. This was lifted in March 1975 but regulated rents have since then been screwed down relatively to other prices in the economy by restrictions on the rate at which rents may be increased. The provisions of the *Housing Finance Act 1972,* which envisaged the gradual decontrol of all properties still held in the vice of the older rent control, have been scrapped by the *Housing Rents and Subsidies Act 1975.* As a sop, landlords of rent-controlled accommodation are now permitted to increase the controlled rent by a proportion of the cost of any repairs.

Rent regulation has been further amended by the 1975 Act. Rent Officers are now required to disregard, in fixing "fair" rents, any improvements (or deterioration) in the amenities of an area since the last rent registration. In time with other instructions to rent officers, 'amenity' is left undefined by the Act. Rent companies complain that registered 'fair' rents average only a half to three-quarters what an open market rent would be. Taken in conjunction with the

March 1975 rules relating to the phasing of any rent increases (increases of over 80 p. (roughly two dollars) a week must be phased over 2 years), this means in effect that rent regulation is failing to provide landlords with gross incomes sufficient to warrant adequate maintenance expenditure.

Even if the 1972 Act generated misgivings, it also offered qualified hope that things might in the end be changed for the better. Possibly there is still hope in the fact that more recent legislation has still retained the idea of housing allowances for needy renters in the private sector. Therein lies the seed of a restoration of a free market in rental housing. But presently it lies on stony ground and the private landlord in Britain is a threatened species more so than ever before.

University of British Columbia
August, 1975.

6

Questions and Some Answers About Rent Control An Empirical Analysis of New York's Experience

EDGAR O. OLSEN

Associate Professor of Economics,
University of Virginia
Visiting Associate Professor,
University of Wisconsin (Madison)

1975

THE AUTHOR

EDGAR O. OLSEN, PhD., is currently Visiting Associate Professor in the Department of Economics at the University of Wisconsin (Madison Campus). Professor Olsen is a native of New Orleans, Louisiana and received his undergraduate training at Tulane University. In 1968 he received his PhD. in Economics from Rice University.

Professor Olsen has written extensively on the theory and practice of housing economics; in particular about housing subsidies and rent control. His publications in scholarly journals include: *A Competitive Theory of the Housing Market, Some Theorems in the Theory of Efficient Transfers,* and *An Econometric Analysis of Rent Control.*

Questions and Some Answers About Rent Control An Empirical Analysis of New York's Experience

EDGAR O. OLSEN

Associate Professor of Economics, University of Virginia
Visiting Associate Professor, University of Wisconsin (Madison)

Introduction

On January 30, 1942, President Roosevelt signed into law the Emergency Price Control Act. The rent control provisions of this law were implemented in New York City (NYC) in November, 1943, setting the maximum rents for all rental dwelling units at their levels of March of that year. The responsibility for rent control in NYC was transferred from the federal to the state government in 1950 and from the state to the city government in 1962. Almost everywhere else in the United States, rent control ended early in the 1950's.

To know the effects of any government program is to know the difference between what did happen in the presence of the program and what would have happened in its absence. Obviously it is no easy matter to know what would have happened in the absence of rent control. Unfortunately, there is no other way to learn about its effects.

This paper summarizes what is known about the effects of rent control in NYC. Although there has been extensive experience with rent control throughout the world, much of the reliable knowledge about its effects refers to NYC. There are several reasons for this. First, good methods for learning about rent control were not developed until the late 1960's and NYC was one of the few cities in the United States having rent control at this time. Secondly, good data for analyzing rent control is available for NYC, and thirdly, at least some members of the city government wanted to know the effects of the program.

In a sense it is misleading to talk about *the effects* of rent control since different rent control ordinances have different provisions and these differences can lead to different results; furthermore, the effects in the first year may be different from the effects in later years. The major provisions of NYC's rent control ordinance are presented in the appendix. Most of the results reported in the paper refer to the effects of the ordinance twenty-five years after its imposition. These caveats should be kept in mind by anyone interested in predicting the effects of a proposed rent control ordinance.

EFFECTS OF RENT CONTROL IN NEW YORK CITY

This section will answer several important questions about rent control based on empirical evidence from NYC. It is essentially a summary of the technical work done by myself and others and represents a fairly exhaustive treatment of available information.

A. Is rent control a solution to a housing shortage?

Rent control is almost always proposed initially as a solution to a housing shortage, the manifestations of which are rapidly rising rents and a low vacancy rate. (Rapidly rising prices of owner-occupied houses are strangely ignored). There is little doubt that in the short-run rent control can slow the rate of increase in rents. However, this does not mean that it is a solution to the problem of inflation. Money that tenants would have spent on housing is spent on other goods and services, driving up their prices. There is no reason to expect the overall rate of inflation to be affected by rent control. Perhaps because this argument is obvious once said, no one has attempted to provide empirical evidence to support it.

In the case of the vacancy rate we are more fortunate. Rent control in NYC must be terminated if the vacancy rate in the controlled sector exceeds five percent. That is, a low vacancy rate in the controlled sector is the official rationale for the continuation of rent control. Obviously, this rationale would make no sense if decontrol would lead to a higher vacancy rate. Table 1 suggests that this is exactly what would happen. In 1940, when neither NYC nor other U.S. cities had rent control ordinances, the vacancy rate in NYC was greater than the vacancy rate in other cities. In 1950, when almost all of these cities were covered by federal rent controls, the vacancy rates were much lower than in 1940 and about the same in NYC as in other cities. By 1960 almost all other cities had long since decontrolled rents, but NYC still had a rent control ordinance. The vacancy rate in NYC was half of that in other cities and the disparity in the rental vacancy rate (2.2% versus 6.2%) was even greater. Furthermore, Table 2 indicates that the vacancy rate in uncontrolled housing in NYC is typically

Table 1 — Combined Renter and Owner Vacancy Rates

	New York City	Other Cities
1940	7.3	4.7
1950	1.1	1.4
1960	2.0	4.0

Notes: In 1940 other cities consisted of all cities of 50,000 inhabitants or more; in 1950 all cities of 100,000 inhabitants or more; in 1960 central cities of all SMSAs.

Sources: Sixteenth Census of the United States: 1940, Table 73.
U.S. Census of Housing: 1950, Table 27.
U.S. Census of Housing: 1960, Tables 9 and 15.

Table 2 — Rental Vaçancy Rates by Control Status in New York City

	1960-1962	1965	1968
Controlled	0.8	2.0	1.0
Single Room Occupancy	7.6	13.0	6.3
Decontrolled	4.3	5.9	2.1
Never controlled	3.9	4.4	0.7

Note: The vacancy rates for 1960-62 were obtained by dividing the number of vacancies in 1962 by the number of available units in 1960.

Sources: Kristoff, pp. 1 and 110; Niebanck, p. 185.

greater than in controlled housing. Therefore, *the evidence from NYC strongly suggests that rent control exacerbates rather than solves a housing shortage.*

B. Should rent control be supported by people who support housing subsidies?

Since many people continue to support rent control decades after it was imposed in response to a temporary shortage, there must be other reasons for their support. I think that many supporters view it as a way of providing housing subsidies.

The purpose of housing subsidies is to induce eligible families to live in better housing than they would occupy if they were given the choice (and equivalent income). A subsidy is tied to housing expenditures and differs from an unrestricted cash grant which is a "no strings attached" income supplement. The principal difference between subsidies and grants is that the former has the objective of forcing the recipient to accept a higher standard of housing while cash grants permit the recipient to choose between housing and other things. The effectiveness of a housing subsidy is judged by the extent to which the subsidy is actually spent on housing.

The basic question, then, is whether or not rent control raises the standard of housing that people occupy? The evidence from NYC suggests that rent control does not produce this result and hence does not attain the primary goal of a housing subsidy program. In separate studies (References 1, 8) using slightly different samples and assumptions, Joseph DeSalvo and I found that, on average, occupants of controlled housing in 1968[1] lived in apartments about as good as the ones that they would have occupied in the absence of rent control.

The studies essentially posed two empirical questions. First, how much would a given family occupying a rent controlled apartment spend on housing in the absence of control? Second, how much would a given controlled apartment rent for in the uncontrolled market? By comparing

[1]The information for these studies was derived from the special New York City Housing and Vacancy Survey undertaken in 1968. This survey collected many pieces of information for about 35,000 housing units.

the answers to these questions we are able to say whether or not persons living in rent controlled apartments would have occupied a more desirable or a less desirable apartment in an uncontrolled market.

In our studies, we used market rent as our measure of the desirability of an apartment. That is, if one apartment would rent for twice as much as another on the uncontrolled market, then we considered the former to be twice as desirable as the latter.

The market rent of the apartment that the family would have occupied in the absence of rent control is the same as the amount that it would have spent on housing if controls had been absent. We predicted this amount for each family in controlled housing by using data on the housing expenditures of families who had the same characteristics and lived in uncontrolled housing. Similarly, we predicted the market rent of each family's controlled apartment by using data on the rents of uncontrolled apartments with similar characteristics.

DeSalvo found that the sum of the predicted market rents exceeded the sum of the predicted housing expenditures by only 1.6 percent; I found that the latter exceeded the former by 4.4 percent. *For the typical family, the benefit of rent control stems from its effect on consumption of non-housing goods and services.* I estimated that, in aggregate, occupants of controlled housing spend 9.9 percent more on non-housing goods and services than they would have spent in the absence of rent control. DeSalvo did not make this comparison.

The only other estimates of these magnitudes, calculated by Elizabeth Roistacher in her doctoral thesis, present a different picture. [*Editor's Note: Although Roistacher's results on this particular issue are different than Olsen's and DeSalvo's, her conclusions are that New York's "rent control has undesirable redistributional effects among tenants of the controlled sector", and that "discrimination against minorities is likely to be more prevalent in a controlled market". She further concludes that "given the social goals of income redistribution, increased housing consumption for lower income households, and the removal of urban decay and related social problems, it is clear that rent control is not an ideal policy for protecting tenants from inflationary rents" (P. 284, Reference 10)*]. Roistacher concludes that the aggregate market rent of controlled units in New York in 1968 was 19.7 percent greater than the aggregate market rent of the apartments that these families would occupy in the absence of rent control and that they spent 8.6 percent more on non-housing goods and services. Unfortunately, her study contains a statistical bias which can be expected to result in an overestimate of the improvement in housing. Specifically, she was able to identify certain controlled units for which it was reasonable to believe that market rents had been underestimated. She adjusted these predictions upward by a reasonable amount. However, she failed to realize that there were certainly other apartments where market rents had been overestimated. Correcting some underestimates, while doing nothing about overestimates, results in an overestimate of the aggregate market rent of controlled units. Therefore, we can only conclude from her study that the improvement in housing is likely to be less than 19.7 percent while the increase in non-housing consumption is in the neighbourhood of 8.6 percent.

In short, the evidence from New York City suggests that rent control causes tenants in the controlled sector to spend most of their resulting increase in disposable income on items other than housing. Consequently, little improvement in their housing condition occurs. Therefore, surprising though it might seem, *no one who favors housing subsidies should support rent controls.*

C. Should people who favor unrestricted cash grants to low-income families favor rent control?

It is often argued that rent control is simply a way of redistributing income from the rich to the poor because landlords are richer than tenants. For this reason rent control is supported by many people who favor unrestricted cash grants to low-income families. Of course, it is not true that every tenant is poorer than his landlord, but even if this were the case, rent control would be a very poor redistributive device.

One important reason is that it distorts consumption patterns substantially. Many occupants of controlled housing live in apartments much less desirable than they would choose if they were given unrestricted cash grants each month, equal to the difference between the market rent and the controlled rent of their apartment, and required to live in uncontrolled housing. Other occupants of controlled housing live in much more desirable apartments.

DeSalvo, Roistacher, and I could have predicted the housing expenditures of families in controlled housing had rent control been replaced by unrestricted cash grants in these amounts. We could then have calculated the difference between this predicted housing expenditure and the predicted market rent of the controlled apartment occupied by each family. The size of this difference indicates the extent of the distortion in a family's consumption pattern. Unfortunately, this comparison did not occur to us. However, I did make another comparison which shows the extent of the distortion.

For each occupant of a controlled apartment, I estimated the annual unrestricted cash grant which, if given to the family in place of the benefits of rent control, would make the family neither better nor worse off than it was under rent control. My estimate of the average cash grant for 1968 is $213. If rent control were equivalent to a program of unrestricted cash grants and hence did not distort consumption patterns, then the average difference between the market and actual rent of controlled apartments would also have been $213. In fact, it was $406. *In other words, the cost of rent control to landlords is about twice its value to tenants.* Rent control is, therefore, a very inefficient redistributive device.

Rent control is not only an inefficient redistributive device but also a grossly inequitable one. There is undoubtedly a great variance in the cost borne by equally wealthy families. Rent control is not limited to low-income families and does not serve all such families. Among families who occupy controlled housing and are similar in many respects, there is an enormous variance in benefits. In short, there is nothing approaching equal treatment of equals under rent control.

While there is no evidence on the distribution of the cost of rent control in NYC, the following propositions are almost certainly true: A) The majority of families at each income level do not own rental housing. B) The cost of rent control is borne overwhelmingly by people who own rental housing. C) Equally wealthy owners of rental property do not bear the same cost because they hold different proportions of their assets in this form.

Two important questions flow from these propositions. 1. Why should rent control, which allegedly serves a public purpose, be financed by an implicit tax on such a small proportion of the population? 2. Why should the magnitude of this tax on equally wealthy people depend upon the proportion of their assets held in the form of rental housing?

Table 3 presents the distribution of income in controlled and uncontrolled housing in NYC in 1968. Clearly, rent control is not limited to low-income families and does not serve all such families.

Table 3 — Distribution of Renter Households in Controlled and Uncontrolled Housing by Income: New York City, 1968

Income of Head and Related Persons	Controlled	Uncontrolled
Under $2000	12.2%	4.1%
2,000-3,999	21.6	9.0
4,000-5,999	22.5	14.8
6,000-7,999	17.3	16.9
8,000-9,999	10.7	15.1
10,000-14,999	10.7	24.6
15,000-24,999	3.8	11.7
25,000 or more	1.0	3.9
TOTAL	100.0	100.0

Source: Lowry, DeSalvo, and Woodfill, p. 249.

Even among families who occupy controlled housing and are the same with respect to income, family size and the age, sex and race of the head of the household, there is an enormous variation in benefits because the excess of market rent over actual rent is different for different controlled units and because some families experience greater distortions in their consumption patterns than other families. I have estimated that the mean benefit for families with average characteristics was $213 during 1968 and that the standard deviation in benefits is $261.

Conclusions

Rent control is a cause of, rather than a solution to, a housing shortage. Unlike housing subsidies it does not result in better housing for its beneficiaries. It is an inefficient and inequitable redistributive device. Even though New York City has had more experience with rent control than any other place in the United States, there are still many unanswered questions concerning its effects in New York. My conclusion from the experience of New York City is that no area should adopt a rent control ordinance unless there is compelling evidence that it will have different effects than the New York City ordinance. This ordinance appears to have no redeeming social value.

APPENDIX
Major Provisions of NYC's Rent Control Ordinance

This appendix provides a summary of the major provisions of NYC's rent control ordinance as of 1968, the year for which major data sources are available. Recently, there have been important changes in the law. However, all of the studies of the effects of rent control in NYC rely on data for 1968 or earlier.

In 1943, virtually all private rental housing in NYC was covered by rent control. By 1968, only 69 percent of such units were covered and the percentage of all units that were owner-occupied had risen from about 16 to 24. The next few paragraphs will describe provisions which influenced this change in the composition of the stock.

When the war ended, dwellings built after February 1, 1947 were exempted from controls, presumably in order to stimulate new construction. By 1968, twenty percent of all private rental units had never been covered by rent control.

Between 1943 and 1968, about 460,000 units were removed from the controlled inventory. About half of these units are now rented in the uncontrolled sector. The numbers of units decontrolled for various reasons are presented in Table 4.

Some of the other half have been converted from renter to owner occupancy. The number of such units is not known but is probably small because there were only 93,000 cooperative and condominium apartments in NYC in 1968 and many of these were undoubtedly never a part of the rental inventory. It appears that no one has sought an explanation for the surprisingly small number of changes in tenure. Certainly, one reason is the occupants of controlled apartments cannot be evicted in order to allow an owner to convert his building into a cooperative or condominium. The rent control ordinance severely limits the grounds on which a tenant may be evicted and for all but a few of these grounds (e.g., nonpayment of rent) the procedures for evicting a tenant are costly and the probability of success is low. Of course, the owner could wait until his units were vacated. However, it is probably difficult to convert some but not all of the apartments in a building to owner occupancy and, if the owner waited until all tenants voluntarily vacated their units, the forgone rental revenues might be substantial.

Table 4 — 1965 Decontrolled Dwellings in NYC
by Reason for Decontrol

	Number	Percentage
Total Decontrolled	199,000	100.0
Apartments in 1 and 2 family houses without businesses that became vacant after May, 1953 and automatically decontrolled	135,000	67.8
Dwellings once part of a larger apartment which was subdivided into smaller units	31,000	15.6
Dwellings occupied by landlord for at least one year and subsequently rented to a tenant	22,000	11.1
High rent decontrol (monthly rent greater than $250)	7,000	3.5
Reason unspecified	4,000	2.0

Source: Rapkin, p. 17.

The other units covered by rent control and not a part of the rental inventory in 1968 were demolished to make way for new residential buildings and non-residential uses. The number of such units is not known. The rate at which this demolition occurred was undoubtedly slowed by the restrictions on evicting tenants.

As a result of new construction, decontrol, demolition, and changes from renter to owner occupancy, the composition of the stock by tenure and control status has changed substantially. Table 5 displays these changes for the 1960's.

The provisions mentioned in the preceding paragraphs concern which units are covered by rent control. Other provisions concern the conditions under which the controlled rent may be changed. Petitions for increases and decreases in maximum rents are handled in the offices of the District Rent Directors. Their decisions may be appealed to the office of the City Rent Administrator and then through the court system. In 1965 the District Rent Offices handled

Table 5 — Available Housing Units in NYC by Tenure and Control Status: 1960, 1965 and 1968
(NUMBERS IN THOUSANDS)

Tenure and Control Status	**Housing Units** 1960		1965		1968	
	Number	**Percent**	**Number**	**Percent**	**Number**	**Percent**
Total	2699	100.0	2792	100.0	2798	100.0
Renter	2115	78.4	2145	76.8	2122	75.8
Controlled	1628	60.3	1476	52.8	1359	48.6
Decontrolled	170	6.3	199	7.1	224	8.0
Never Controlled	207	7.7	333	11.9	395	14.1
Public Housing	111	4.1	138	4.9	144	5.2
Owner	583	21.6	647	23.2	676	24.2
Homeowner	n.a.	n.a.	570	20.4	583	20.8
Cooperative	n.a.	n.a.	77	2.7	93	3.3

Note: n.a. refers to data which are not available.

Source: Niebanck, p. 28.

about 660,000 cases. About one percent of these cases were appealed to the City Rent Administrator and 600 of these cases were brought up for court review.

The major provision accounting for increases in controlled rents allows tenants to voluntarily agree to a two-year lease calling for a rent increase of up to 15 percent. Almost all such agreements occur when a family is trying to obtain occupancy of a vacant controlled apartment. Even with an increase in rent, most of these apartments are bargains for many families compared with the alternative of renting in the uncontrolled sector. Since the landlord is free to choose his tenants, he is able to get these families to agree to an increase in the controlled rent. In the 1960's, about half of the dollar value of the increases in controlled rents was attributable to this provision. The numbers and average amounts of rent increases for other reasons are shown in Table 6.

Table 6 — Selected NYC Rent Changes Granted from May 1, 1962, through December 31, 1968

	Number of Units with Rent Changes	Average Monthly Dollar Payment	Average Percent Adjustment
Selected Increases Granted			
Total for improvements	1,350,823	4.83	6.5
Increased Services or Facilities	955,246	5.22	7.1
Major Capital Improvements	168,070	4.13	5.6
Substantial Rehabilitation	227,500	3.84	4.8
Other	7	2.00	3.3
Total for Costs	84,263	10.26	10.1
Net Annual Return	82,413	10.23	10.2
Increased Costs: Small Structures, Hotels, etc.	1,850	11.48	7.4
Selected Decreases Granted			
Total, Painting and other Services	1,005,731	10.53	17.4

Source: Niebanck, p. 124.

A tenant is entitled to a rent reduction if there is any decrease in essential services (such as refrigerators, stoves and heating), if equipment is not maintained, or if the building seriously deteriorates. There are detailed provisions concerning how often the landlord must paint. Table 6 contains the number and average amount of rent decreases granted. About half of the tenant applications for rent decreases are settled by the landlord restoring services. A fourth are denied.

Finally, as a condition for renting an apartment, it is illegal for a landlord or superintendent to (1) accept a cash bonus, (2) accept any gift of value, rental fee, or commission, (3) require a new tenant to buy furniture, (4) charge the rate for a furnished apartment if the tenant has been permitted to bring in his own furniture, or (5) require more than one month's rent as a security deposit.

SOURCES

1. DeSalvo, Joseph S. "Reforming Rent Control in New York City: Analysis of Housing Expenditures and Market Rentals." *Papers and Proceedings of the Regional Science Association,* Vol. 27, 1970, pp. 195-227.

2. Kristoff, Frank S. *People, Housing and Rent Control in New York City.* The City of New York, City Rent and Rehabilitation Administration, June 1964.

3. Lowry, Ira S., ed. *Confronting the Crisis.* Vol. 1 of *Rental Housing in New York City.* RM-6190-NYC New York: The New York City-Rand Institute, February 1970.

4. Lowry, Ira S.; DeSalvo, Joseph S.; and Woodfill, Barbara M. *The Demand for Shelter.* Vol. 2 of *Rental Housing in New York City.* R-649-NYC. New York: The New York City-Rand Institute, June 1971.

5. Moorhouse, John Charles. "Optimal Housing Maintenance under Rent Control." Unpublished doctoral dissertation, Northwestern University, 1969.

6. New York Rent and Rehabilitation Administration. *The New Little Book on Rent Control.* The City of New York, Rent and Rehabilitation Administration, 1965.

7. Niebanck, Paul L. *Rent Control and The Rental Housing Market: New York City 1968.* The City of New York, Housing and Development Administration, Department of Rent and Housing Maintenance, January 1970.

8. Olsen, Edgar O. "An Econometric Analysis of Rent Control." *Journal of Political Economy,* Vol. 80, Nov./Dec. 1972, pp. 1081-1100.

9. Rapkin, Chester, *The Private Rental Housing Market in New York City, 1965.* The City of New York, City Rent and Rehabilitation Administration, December 1966.

10. Roistacher, Elizabeth Anne. "The Distribution of Tenant Benefits under Rent Control." Unpublished doctoral dissertation, University of Pennsylvania, 1972.

11. U.S. Bureau of the Census. *Sixteenth Census of the United States: 1940. Housing.* Vol. 2, *General Characteristics.* Part 1: *United States Summary.* U.S. Government Printing Office, Washington, D.C., 1943.

12. U.S. Bureau of the Census. *U.S. Census of Housing: 1950.* Vol. 1, *General Characteristics.* Part I; *U.S. Summary.* U.S. Government Printing Office, Washington, D.C., 1953.

13. U.S. Bureau of the Census. *U.S. Census of Housing: 1960.* Vol. 1, *States and Small Areas. United States Summary.* Final Report HC(1)-1. U.S. Government Printing Office, Washington, D.C., 1963.

7

The Rise and Fall of Swedish Rent Control

SVEN RYDENFELT

Lecturer in Economics, University of Lund, Sweden

1975

THE AUTHOR

SVEN RYDENFELT was born in 1911; at university 1934-36; teacher's training college 1936-38. He was a secondary school teacher, 1938-45, returning to university after the war to study and teach, becoming a Doctor of Economics in 1954. Since 1961 he has been a lecturer in economics with tenure for life at the University of Lund.

His publications include his doctoral dissertation, *Communism in Sweden* (1954), books and articles on rent control and housing policy, as well as other socio-economic subjects.

The Rise and Fall of Swedish Rent Control

SVEN RYDENFELT

Lecturer in Economics,
University of Lund,
Sweden

'Economics does not say that isolated government interference with the prices of only one commodity or a few commodities is unfair, bad, or unfeasible. It says that such interference produces results contrary to its purpose, that it makes conditions worse, not better, *from the point of view of the government and those backing its interference.*'

LUDWIG VON MISES[1]

I. A 'TEMPORARY' EMERGENCY REGULATION MADE PERMANENT

When rent control was introduced in Sweden in 1942 in accordance with almost unanimous support in Parliament, the decision was founded on a conviction that it was an emergency regulation that would be abolished as fast as possible after the Second World War. It was believed that war-time inflation would be followed by a deflation with sharp declines in prices, as happened after the First World War.

However, the strong deflation which followed the First World War did not recur after the Second. For this reason rents in Sweden after 1945 remained at a level far below the prices of other commodities. And while rental costs of apartment houses remained for a long time almost unchanged, salaries and wages rose rapidly, as Table 1 demonstrates.

[1]Human Action: A Treatise on Economics, Yale University Press, New Haven 1949, p. 758.

Table 1 — Rental Costs and Wages (Sweden 1939-1975)

	1939	1942	1945	1950	1960	1970	1975	Average Annual Rate of Growth
Rental Costs (1942=100)	83	100	103	104	166	253	370	4.2%
Wages (1942=100)	80	100	108	162	391	917	1600	8.7%

Sources: 'Rental costs': rents, fuel and light based on the cost-of-living index of the Board of Social Welfare. 'Wages': paid to workers in industry, communications, public services, etc., based on the statistics of the Board of Social Welfare. The 1975 figures are preliminary.

In spite of all the good intentions to abolish rent control soon after the war it succeeded in surviving until 1975, when its last remnants were finally removed (350,000 out of 2,000,000 housing units in apartment houses). The moral is that rent control is easy to introduce but hard to abolish.

A housing shortage develops

To the economist, it seems self-evident that a price control like the Swedish rent control must lead to a demand surplus, that is, a housing shortage. For a long period the general public was more inclined to believe that the shortage was a result of the abnormal situation created by the war, and this even in a non-participating country like Sweden. The defenders of rent control were quick to adopt the opinion held by the general public. All attempts by critics to point to rent control as the villain in the housing drama were firmly rejected.

The foremost defender of rent control in Sweden was for many years Alf Johansson, Director-General of the Royal Board of Housing, who has been called 'the father of the Swedish housing policy'. In an article in 1948 he described the development of the housing shortage thus:

> 'An acute shortage of housing units developed as early as 1941. In the following year the shortage was general and reached approximately 50,000 units in the urban communities, i.e., somewhat more than the house construction during a boom year'.[2]

[2]Svensk sparbankstidskrift, No. 2, 1948.

In a lecture he described the situation in 1948 as follows:

> 'We have the same shortage as at the end of the war, but the situation has not deteriorated in spite of a very great increase in demand'.[3]

According to Mr. Johansson's rough sketch, the housing shortage in Sweden reached its peak as early as 1942 — 50,000 dwellings — and remained practically unchanged in the following years.

The actual development was quite different, as was revealed in the reports of the Public Dwelling Exchange offices. Only Malmö — the third largest city — had an exchange of this kind during the early war years; its reports provide a detailed account of the development (Table 2).

Table 2 — Development of Housing Shortage in Malmö, 1940-1973

		APPLICANTS	
	Vacancies	**Total**	**Without a Dwelling**
1940	1,144	—	58
1941	1,047	—	129
1942	593	—	138
1943	165	—	205
1944	44	301	247
1945	41	390	288
1946	22	323	221*
1947	8	539	418
1948	—	2,409	1,698
1949	—	6,693	3,472
1950	—	9,939	4,803
1960	—	24,901	4,254
1970	—	34,478	10,660
1973	2,086	40,326	11,343

Source: Reports of the Dwelling Exchange Office.

*In 1946 all 'old' applications were deleted from the records and a new 'purge' is going on in 1975.

Stockholm, the capital of Sweden, opened a Dwelling Exchange Office for the first time in 1947. Its reports give an illuminating picture of a rapidly deteriorating situation in the housing market. Families with two children, which in

[3]From the minutes of the Congress of the Swedish Real Estate Owners' Association in Malmö.

1950 obtained a housing unit through the Exchange Office, experienced an average waiting time of nine months. The development during the following years is shown in Table 3.

Table 3 — Average Waiting Period for Dwellings in Stockholm

	Months		Months
1950	9	1954	26
1951	15	1955	23
1952	21	1956	30
1953	24	1957	35
		1958	40

Source: Reports of the Dwelling Exchange Office. The series was not continued after 1958.

Conclusion

Thus, the 'popular opinion' encouraged by defenders of rent control, that the Swedish housing shortage was a product of the war, does not accord with the evidence demonstrated either by the Malmö data or the Stockholm data. In fact, all of the data indicate that the shortage during the war years was insignificant compared with that after the war. It was only in the post-war rent control era that the housing shortage assumed such proportions that it became Sweden's most serious social problem.

II. HOUSING AND POPULATION

The rapidly increasing housing shortage after 1945 soon ripened into a situation which could no longer be attributed to the supply dislocations that were supposedly created by the war. New explanations were needed. That most commonly adopted by the general public was the assumption that the shortage was a consequence of insufficient construction activity. If population increased at a faster rate than the number of housing units, there was bound to be a shortage, people thought; and they therefore adopted the untested assumption that construction was lagging behind. Among the defenders of rent control this population growth explanation became for a long time the most fashionable.

Fallacy of the population growth explanation

The defenders of rent control were anxious to emphasize that special consideration must be given to the rise in the marriage rate after 1940, since most housing units are occupied by married couples. The following quotation from an article by Mr. Johansson is significant:

> 'During 1945-46 the number of marriages in the cities was 50 percent higher than the average for the 1930's. Under such conditions it is not difficult to explain why the addition of new housing units, even though large, has been absorbed and the shortage left unaltered'.[4]

Let us confront this "model" with statistical data on housing and population (Table 4).

Table 4 — Housing and Population in Sweden, 1940-1975

	No. of Housing Units	Total Population	No. of married couples	Number of dwellings per 100 inhabitants	Number of dwellings per 100 married couples
1940	1,960,000	6,371,000	1,330,000	31	147
1945	2,102,000	6,674,000	1,463,000	32	144
1960	2,675,000	7,498,000	1,783,000	36	150
1965	2,875,000	7,773,000	1,869,000	37	154
1970	3,180,000	8,080,000	1,927,000	39	165
1975	3,480,000	8,200,000	1,975,000	42	175

Sources: Number of housing units in 1940 according to official estimates in SOU 1945: Table 63, p. 228; data for other years from official censuses. The 1975 figures are preliminary.

During the war years the rate of housing construction was relatively low, but still high enough to increase, marginally, the number of housing units per 100 inhabitants. The number of housing units per 100 married couples, however, declined slightly (from 147 to 144) due to the exceptionally high marriage rate during the war years. During the years after 1945, when the big shortage developed, the number of dwellings in Sweden increased at a considerably faster rate than both the total population and the number of married couples.

[4]Svensk sparbankstidskrift, op. cit.

Conclusion

In the light of the above data it seemed sensible to reject the explanation that the housing shortage was a crisis product of the war years. We have now found that the population explanation does not stand the test either.

Theory and forecasting

Human life is a walk into a future filled with uncertainty. The purpose of science is to illuminate, like a searchlight, the road in front of us. Therefore, the touchstone of all knowledge is its ability to anticipate the future — the forecast. When our astronomers can forecast hundreds of years ahead the moment for an eclipse of the sun, they prove that their conception of reality, their "model" of the universe, is a realistic one.

The famous sociologist, Florian Znaniecki, has expressed this thesis in the following way:

> 'Foresight of the future is the most conclusive test of the validity of scientific theories, a test perfected in experimental science. "Prediction" is thus the essential link between theory and practice'.[5]

The need for knowledge and forecasts about society is far stronger in a centrally-directed 'planned' economy than in a liberal market economy. The British economist, Sir Roy Harrod, has formulated this conclusion in the following terms:

> 'Lack of economic comprehension may not matter so much if the system is largely self-working. But when the working of the machine necessitates the constant vigilance of the supervisor, and the supervisor does not understand the mechanism, there is bound to be serious trouble'.[6]

Judging from different forecasts, the decision-makers behind the Swedish rent controls had highly imperfect knowledge about the structure and function of the housing market. For several years they thought that the housing shortage was a product of the war and for many years

[5]Proximate Future of Sociology: Controversies in Doctrine and Method, American Journal of Sociology, May 1945 p. 516.

[6]Britain Must Put Her House in Order, World Review, December 1951, p. 13.

afterwards they thought it to be a product of population changes. From such models of the housing market they made very optimistic forecasts, according to which the shortage after the war would quickly disappear.

The following 'forecast' shows how Sweden's leading official expert on housing policy 'anticipated' future developments as of 1944:

> 'The liquidation of the housing market shortage is a once-for-all business, which ought to be accomplished in a relatively short time, though not over so short a period as one year.'[7]

As we have seen, subsequent developments were very much different.

A forecast of an entirely different nature was published by Professor Eli F. Heckscher, at that time the doyen of Swedish economic history and economics:

> 'It is probably a general opinion that the housing shortage is due to insufficient construction activity. But this is, by and large, an enormous mistake. In a free housing market no shortage would exist at the present rate of construction. On the other hand, no rate of construction activity can eliminate the shortage under the present order. It is like the tub of the Danaids, from which water was constantly flowing out at a faster rate than it could be poured in'.[8]

I myself, published a similar forecast a few months earlier:

> 'The cause of the housing shortage is to be found entirely on the demand side. As a consequence of rent control and the relative reduction of the rent — the manipulated low price — demand has increased to such an extent that an ever-widening gap between supply and demand has developed in spite of the high level of construction activity. Our great mistake is that we always seek the cause of a shortage on the supply side, while it is as frequently to be found on the demand side. The housing shortage will be our companion forever,

[7]Alf Johansson in Ett genombrott, 1944 (a dedication volume in honour of Gustav Möller, Minister of Social Affairs).

[8]Dagens Nyheter, 15 May, 1948.

unless we prevent demand from running ahead of production'.[9]

It will be convenient to conclude this section with a now-classical statement by the late Professor Frank H. Knight, the 'grand old man' of the Chicago School of Economics:

> 'If educated people can't or won't see that fixing a price below the market level inevitably creates a "shortage" (and one above a "surplus"), it is hard to believe in the usefulness of telling them anything whatever in this field of discourse'.[10]

III. SINGLE PEOPLE INVADE THE HOUSING MARKET

> 'You need not eat the whole egg to feel it is rotten'
> Russian proverb.

As indicated in Table 4 the number of housing units in Sweden during the period 1940 to 1975 rose by 1,520,000 (net), while the number of married couples increased by only 645,000. Even if every married couple had obtained their own home, there would still have been 875,000 dwellings available for other groups.

Table 5 — Number of Persons by Groups and Percentage Occupying Own Dwellings

	Married couples	%	Previously married persons	%	Unmarried adults	%
1940	1,330,000	98	435,000	65	1,453,000	23
1945	1,463,000	98	457,000	65	1,337,000	25
1960	1,783,000	98	575,000	75	1,047,000	36
1965	1,869,000	98	628,000	77	1,051,000	43
1970	1,927,000	98	717,000	80	1,073,000	50
1975	1,975,000	98	815,000	82	1,300,000	55

Sources: Official housing and population censuses. The 1975 figures are preliminary.

Note: The sum total of *occupied* dwellings, calculated from Table 5 is not equal to the sum total of housing units in Table 4. At every time, even during shortage periods, there is a reserve of unoccupied empty dwellings. According to the housing census this reserve was 93,000 in 1965 and 129,000 in 1970.

[9] Handelstidningen, 16 December, 1947.

[10] Truth and Relevance at Bay, American Economic Review, December 1949, P. 1,274.

Which are the groups in Swedish society that have increased their occupation of dwelling space to such an extent that a serious shortage has developed? There are three groups of consumers in the housing market: married couples, previously married people (widows, widowers and the divorced), and unmarried adults (20 years or older). Table 5 shows the size of each group at various years and the percentage living in dwellings (houses or flats) of their own.

Growth of demand among unmarried adults

All housing censuses indicate that, with few exceptions, married couples have always occupied housing units of their own. However, it is also true — even in a free housing market — that there is some 'doubling up'; for example, young married couples living with their parents for a while. The majority (65 per cent) of the previously married also lived in dwellings of their own in 1940. Their share had increased by 17 per cent by 1975.

The only dramatic change has been for unmarried adults of whom only one in four occupied a dwelling of his own in 1940, while 35 years later more than one in two did. Thus the supply of dwellings available for unmarried adults must have rapidly improved during the 35-year period (Table 6, which is another way of viewing the information contained in Table 5).

Table 6 — Persons without Dwellings of their Own
(In Absolute and Relative Numbers, 1940-1975)

	Married Couples	%	Previously Married	%	Unmarried Adults	%
1940	27,000	2	152,000	35	1,119,000	77
1945	29,000	2	160,000	35	1,003,000	75
1960	36,000	2	144,000	25	708,000	64
1965	37,000	2	144,000	23	611,000	57
1970	39,000	2	143,000	20	592,000	50
1975	39,000	2	147,000	18	585,000	45

Sources: Official housing and population censuses. The 1975 figures are preliminary.

Table 6 shows that in both 1940 and 1945 over 1 million unmarried adults lacked housing units of their own. The reason why the housing shortage — the demand surplus — was relatively small as late as 1945 in spite of this enormous reserve of demand was that only a small proportion of these persons were actively seeking dwellings of their own. The majority either lived — and were satisfied to live — with their parents, or they rented furnished rooms.

The majority of unmarried adults from the beginning accepted a passive role. The explanation of the housing shortage must be sought in the fact that this majority was later progressively transformed into active dwelling-seekers who invaded the housing market and with energy and success hunted and occupied homes. As indicated in Table 5, the share of residents with own dwellings in this group has increased from 23 per cent in 1940 to 55 per cent in 1975. The implication of this strongly-increased demand for dwellings among unmarried adults is that they occupied 416,000 more homes than they would have done had only the same proportion (23 per cent) as in 1940 occupied their own dwellings. As the number of dwellings in Sweden increased by a net 1,520,000 from 1940 to 1975 more than 25 per cent of the increase has thus been disposed of exclusively to satisfy the extra demand of unmarried adults.

What has brought about this upsurge in the demand of single persons for private dwellings? The reason of course is that the normal relation between income and rents has been entirely distorted by rent control. In the period 1942 to 1975 industrial wages grew to 16 times what they were in 1942 while rents less than quadrupled. The distortion was particularly marked between income and rents of apartment houses built before 1942 (see Table 1).

That the share of persons with housing units of their own in the unmarried adult group increased from 23 per cent in 1940 to 55 per cent in 1975 by no means implies that the demand for dwellings by this group was satisfied. The longest queue at the housing exchange offices was, during all the shortage years, made up of unmarried adults.

Responsiveness of housing demand to changes in price

Would not a strong reduction in the rent-income ratio have occurred even in the absence of rent control and the demand for dwellings have increased as a consequence? Certainly, but the demand increase would have been less accentuated and, in particular, it would have been less among unmarried adults. It all depends on the "price elasticity" of demand. According to common experience, the price and income elasticity of demand for dwellings is low, as it is for other necessities like food and clothing. ‡It is on this basis that the supporters of rent control have attempted to build up a defence. If the demand for dwellings has a low elasticity, they argue, a relative reduction in rent levels could not have increased demand very much.

This general reasoning, however, is valid only for the married and previously married groups. For members of these groups private dwellings are a necessity and, as a result, price and income elasticities are relatively low. The situation is different for unmarried adults. For the majority in this group a self-contained housing unit is somewhat of a luxury, a non-necessity. Young people will often hesitate if they have the choice between going on living cheaply and comfortably with their parents or moving out and acquiring a dwelling of their own.

That unmarried adults occupy self-contained housing units of their own to a lesser extent than the married is not due to lower income. In fact, a comparison of income levels, taking account of the obligations of family men — that is, the number of persons living on one income — shows that the incomes of unmarried adults are as high as those of the married. The unmarried have demanded dwellings to a lesser extent because they assign a higher priority to other things, such as clothing, amusements, travel, education, etc.

For the majority of unmarried adults a dwelling is a relatively dispensable commodity, and the demand for a commodity of this kind is normally highly sensitive to changes in price or income. The strong reduction in rents relative to other prices and to incomes (resulting from rent

‡Editor's note: Price (or income) elasticity of demand for a commodity is high if a given percentage change in price (or income) leads to a greater percentage change in the quantity demanded. Elasticity is low if the quantity demanded changes less (in percentage terms) than the change in price or income.

control) has, for this reason, considerably stimulated the demand for homes on the part of unmarried adults.

The data in Table 6 indicate that in 1945 more than a million unmarried adults in Sweden lacked housing units of their own. This represented a very large potential demand reserve that rent control unleashed on the housing market. The influx of this group into the housing market naturally created a demand which far exceeded supply.

IV. HOUSING PRODUCTION GROSS AND NET

> 'In many cases rent control appears to be the most efficient technique presently known to destroy a city — except for bombing.'
>
> Assar Lindbeck[11]

Deterioration of the housing stock

It is well known and documented that rent controls result in poorer maintenance, fewer renovations and modernisations and, therefore, in the long run in a serious deterioration in the quality of dwellings. Because some requests for rent increases have been granted, the defenders of control have persistently contended that deterioration and slum development have not occurred. This argument is fallacious.

Rent control breeds slums

As a result of control and lower rental income, owners' ability to maintain their apartment houses has declined. In particular, their incentive for such upkeep which is motivated by an aesthetic or comfort point of view has dwindled.

In a free market there is always a surplus of dwellings and flats to let. If the owner in such a market does not keep his property in good condition he runs the risk of losing his tenants and being left with empty flats and losses in rental income. In a controlled market with severe shortages, the owner is under no such compulsion. However badly maintained his property, there are always long queues of homeless people willing to rent his shabby, poorly maintained flats.

[11] *The Political Economy of the New Left*, 1970 (Harper & Row, 1972). Lindbeck, a professor of economics in Stockholm is, like Professors Oskar Lange and Abba P. Lerner, both a socialist and (partly) a supporter of a market economy.

Since there is no economic incentive to encourage the owners to repair, even basic upkeep, which in the long run is necessary to prevent serious quality deterioration (i.e. slums), is neglected. A development of this kind is difficult to describe in quantitative terms. But thanks to the detailed Swedish statistics on the number of new dwellings and the periodic housing censuses, an important aspect of the process can be documented (Table 7).

Table 7 — Gross and Net Housing Production, 1941-45 to 1971-75

	Total new dwellings constructed (a)	Net increase in stock of dwellings (gain) (b)	Dwellings removed from housing stock (loss) (c)	'Loss Ratio' of (c) to (a) %
1941-45	180,000	142,000	38,000	20
1946-60	825,000	573,000	252,000	30
1961-65	415,000	200,000	215,000	52
1966-70	515,000	306,000	209,000	41
1971-75	465,000	298,000	167,000	36

Sources: *Housing Construction* (Swedish Official Statistics), and the housing censuses. Figures for 1971-75 are preliminary.

Rapid 'loss' of houses

What is striking about Table 7 is the rapid increase in the 'loss' (column C) up to the year 1965. During the period 1941 to 1945 the net increase in the stock of dwellings was about 80 per cent of new production and the 'loss' only 20 per cent. During the years 1961 to 1965, the net addition was barely 50 per cent and the 'loss' more than 50 per cent. The 'loss' in those years assumed such proportions that the authorities appointed a special committee with instructions to try to explain 'the mystery of the disappearing dwellings'. After 1965 the process of decontrol got into full swing, and from 1965 to 1970 the number of controlled private houses decreased from 900,000 to 600,000 and from 1970 to 1975 from 600,000 to 350,000. As a consequence, the number of 'losses' decreased.

The anticipation of profits is the incentive to private enterprise to produce housing units. If this incentive is destroyed by regulations, and if it is made more profitable for the owner of apartment houses to rent his dwellings for commercial purposes, then it is not possible to prevent — in spite of prohibitions — a conversion of dwellings to offices, shops or storerooms.

It was of no avail to pour increasing amounts of public funds into the housing bag, as long as we did not patch up its holes. It was of no avail that since 1945 we had built more dwellings per head in Sweden than in any other country (according to the *UN Statistical Yearbook*). It was of no avail that we built more than 100,000 dwellings per year, when the 1967-1972 annual 'loss' at the same time was about 40,000. A construction of 70,000 dwellings and a loss of 10,000 would have given us the same net addition. The system of control obviously caused an enormous and shameful waste of resources.

V. FAREWELL TO RENT CONTROL

In the seventies there has been something of a housing revolution in Sweden. The gradual abolition of rent control since 1958 — when council houses were exempted — has meant a gradual reduction in the housing shortage, and in the seventies the shortage has been replaced by a surplus. In the face of a growing surplus the rate of construction has decreased from an all-time record of 110,000 dwelling units in 1970 to 70,000 in 1975. The last remnants of rent control were removed in 1975. Some glimpses of this somewhat surprising development will be presented here.

Council housing

Since 1932 Sweden has had social-democratic governments with an antipathy towards private housing, whether privately-owned apartment houses or owner-occupied single family houses. The construction of council houses, owned by local authorities, and cooperative houses, owned by building societies, has been encouraged by special concessions and subsidies, and as a consequence, out of 2,000,000 rented dwellings in 1975, 600,000 are in council houses and 500,000 in cooperative houses.

The government apparently believed that apartments in local authorities' projects would be cheaper, due to the absence of profits, and better than privately-owned apartments. The managers of the local authorities' projects — often with a political career as their only merit — energetically tried to live up to that hope. But, costs could not be conjured away. In the event, rents on the council apartments stayed, for a time, at about the same level as the rents on private apartments.

Political pressures ultimately had their effect however, and for a number of years council project managers set rents lower than were to be found in private housing. This was done in spite of the fact that at the lower level rents did not cover costs. Gradually this policy led to a depletion of council project funds and they had to fight desperately against growing liquidity problems. In the face of such difficulties there was only one expedient — rent increases. And, as council houses had been freed from rent controls in 1958, rents were increased. Having allowed considerable increases in the rents on council houses, the government had to allow private rent increases also.

Cooperative housing

In Sweden, building societies own about 500,000 housing units in apartment houses. Nominally, these houses are owned by cooperative societies founded by cooperating families, but in reality these flats — with certain restrictions — are owner-occupied.

In 1939 only 4 per cent of new construction was built by the societies, but during the war years and the following decades cooperative housing was so encouraged by the government that the share of cooperative housing in 1959 reached a peak of 32 per cent. In subsequent years the share of cooperative housing has been declining and in 1975 the share is less than 10 per cent. Why?

Because special concessions by government are not enough, there must also be a shortage for a scheme of this sort to be successful. The gradual abolition of rent control from 1958 meant that the shortage reached its maximum proportions about that time. With gradually shrinking queues, the market for cooperative housing deteriorated year after year.

In order to become a member of a cooperative housing society a person must pay a rather large sum in cash, and in a shortage situation people had no choice. But as the market was permitted, by the return to economic pricing, to provide a supply of alternatives, a preference for rented apartments in the private sector and for single-family houses became evident. The demand for cooperative houses shrank to such an extent that it often happened that a family wanting to move could not find another family willing to take over and pay that sum in cash that they themselves had paid. As the risks of such losses became generally known, the demand for cooperative flats shrank still more.

There is a class of organisms called "pathophiles" that detest healthy environments but thrive on sick plants and animals. So it is with council and cooperative housing enterprises. They had their golden age during the years when our housing market was fatally ill and disorganized by government regulations and shortage. But the more the shortage decreased and the more the market recovered its balance the more the status of these enterprises deteriorated.

Private housing enterprises, on the contrary, thrive only in healthy, balanced markets and react with pronounced "pathophobia" against pathological environments. During the worst control — and shortage — years, private housing suffered seriously.

From shortage to surplus

As rent control was gradually abolished, the queues grew shorter and vacancies began to emerge. But it was not until 1970 that a considerable surplus — mostly municipal and cooperative — developed. For these housing enterprises this surplus was a shocking experience. They had for several decades lived in a world without vacancies, a world they found natural. In their economic calculations there was no allowance — and no funds — for the losses associated with vacancies.

For municipal and cooperative housing enterprises this was an abnormal and undesirable phenomenon meaning economic catastrophe, and in 1972 the situation for both the municipal and the cooperative housing enterprises was so disastrous that the government had to hasten to their rescue.

Bankruptcies would have meant political scandal and 1973 was an election year.

So, loans on extremely advantageous conditions were given, and the local governments — the legal owners of the council houses — had to provide extensive subsidies as well. Up to 1975, vacancies — and vacancy losses — have grown year by year, and with them the need for loans. Most of the borrowing enterprises are in such a precarious financial condition that there is little likelihood that they will be able to repay the interest on the loans, let alone the capital values. The losses, therefore, will be paid by the taxpayers.

New construction

The Swedish Government in 1965 made a bold promise according to which one million new dwellings would be built during the decade 1965-1974. Until then the hunger for new dwellings had seemed insatiable, and the Government did not provide for the possibility of a surplus of housing. Thanks to an over-dimensioned building industry and extensive subsidies, the over-ambitious programme could be fulfilled.

The gradual abolition of rent control plus extensive new construction laid the base for a surplus that from 1970 became really distressing. But a political "promise" is a "promise" and in spite of growing surpluses the building programme had to be fulfilled. A Swedish construction record — 110,000 new dwelling units — was reached in 1970, after which construction went on at a decreasing rate. In 1971 construction was 107,000; in 1972-104,000; in 1973-97,000 and in 1974-85,000. In 1975 it will be about 70,000.

According to our socialist Swedish Government, housing construction must be controlled in order to prevent the ups and downs of private unregulated production. But in spite of strict control, construction in Sweden went down from 110,000 to 70,000 dwelling units in five years. And in 1976 — according to starting statistics — new construction will probably be no more than 55,000; which means a decrease of 50 per cent in six years!

Swedish Socialist Governments in recent decades have been hostile towards owner-occupied single-family houses — an "individualistic middle class" sort of housing. So, new construction of such houses was restricted. In the fifties the share of single-family housing in total construction reached a low of 20 per cent and still in 1970 the share was less than 30 per cent.

But the surplus of apartments was growing rapidly and new construction could not go on as usual, and so, the number of new apartments decreased from 75,000 in 1970 to about 22,000 in 1975. The building workers, however, had to be employed and the construction of single-family houses was the only alternative. And so at a growing scale, owner-occupied single-family homes were substituted for apartments. The market for single-family houses having been undersupplied for decades, the demand for such homes seemed insatiable. And so the share in 1972 rose to 36 per cent, in 1973 to 45 and in 1974 to 55. And according to housing starts statistics, the share in 1975 will reach 65 per cent!

During the shortage years, apartments of low quality in dismal environments were mass-produced. And having no choice, the homeless families in the queues had to accept them. The growing surpluses, however, created quite a new situation; the seller's market was transformed into a buyer's market. The housing enterprises had to compete for the tenants, and this competition forced the builders to use all their creativity to produce attractive flats. During the shortage years they could ignore the wants and wishes of the consumers but now they had to respond to them.

Fewer "skyscrapers" are built, and more construction in Sweden now consists of low houses with one or two stories and with an easy and intimate contact with the ground. Most families have out-of-door-rooms or green plots of their own. As a matter of fact, the changed market situation changed the quality of new construction — houses and environment — in a miraculous way. Because of inflation and rising costs, new flats must be more expensive than old ones, and so in a balanced market they can find tenants only if they are more attractive. The builders in Sweden, accustomed to the protection that shortages provide, are today adjusting without grace to consumer sovereignty. A development made possible by the return to a market situation!

The role of Swedish tenants

About 650,000 Swedes are members of The Tenants' Association, from the beginning fanatical defenders of rent control. But the experiences of the controls were so disheartening that some ten years ago the association changed its policy and began lobbying for repeal of the controls.

As a matter of fact there are special factors behind this surprising policy transformation. Rents in Sweden — like wages — are now decided after negotiations between The Tenants' Association and The Landlords' Association. The biggest single landlord negotiator at the bargaining table is The Local Authorities Association with 600,000 flats, and as is well-known, this bargaining partner's enterprises, in 1975, are balancing at the verge of bankruptcy. The tenant negotiators therefore, have to accept considerable rent increases annually. And in doing so they have to accept equivalent increases in the rents for private apartment houses.

The Swedish housing situation of the seventies is, then, something of a paradox. The owners of 600,000 "nationalized" flats, the local authorities, function as a very strong pressure group — with political backing in the Government — to secure rent increases near to or above what a free market would have provided. And because of the bargaining strength of the local authorities, private landlords have got equivalent increases. And so the Swedish housing market of today — in spite of remaining regulations — functions more like a free market than a controlled one.

VI. RENT CONTROL — DREAM AND REALITY

> 'Rent control has in certain western countries constituted, maybe, the worst example of poor planning by governments lacking courage and vision'.
>
> Gunnar Myrdal‡

Good intentions confounded

1. 'It is not for single persons that we have created our housing policy but in order to give families better dwellings'.[12]

The ignorance of the authorities about the mechanism of the housing market explains their inability to lead development in the directions they themselves desire. They never wanted their policy to favour unmarried adults. Judging from the practical results, however, one is led to believe that favouritism of this kind has been the primary objective. Earlier we showed how the share of unmarried adults with their own dwellings has increased from 23 to 55 percent.

Unmarried adults have increasingly been given the opportunity to invade the housing market and occupy a gradually increasing share of homes. At the same time, tens of thousands of families with children have been unable to find homes of their own.

A free housing market always has a surplus — an available reserve of empty apartments. We call such a market a buyer's market because the buyer has the upper hand. The normal situation in such a market can be said to be that a hundred landlords compete for each tenant. In such a market even a poor family has opportunities of finding and renting a flat. According to a housing census from the free market of 1940 (Table 5), 98 per cent of all married couples then had dwellings of their own. In such a market, landlords often have the choice between only two alternatives —

‡Editor's Note: Gunnar Myrdal co-winner, with F.A. Hayek, of the 1974 Nobel Prize in Economics, was described by Prof. Paul Samuelson, himself a Nobel Winner in 1970, as follows: "Dr. Myrdal has been anything but a believer in laissez-faire, having been an important architect of the Swedish Labor Party's welfare state". The New York Times, October 10, 1974.

[12]Statement by Gustav Möller in the 1st Chamber of the Parliament, 20 January 1951. At that time Moller was Minister of Social Affairs and had the principal responsibility for housing policy.

to leave flats empty or to accept poor families with children as tenants. Under such conditions the latter alternative is often chosen.

A deficit market, on the other hand, is always a seller's market. The normal situation in the tight Swedish housing market was that a hundred homeless potential tenants competed for every vacant dwelling. These hundred included both families with children and single persons. Heavily squeezed between the demands of tenants for repairs on the one hand and reduced rental income due to rent control on the other, it is understandable that landlords in many cases showed a preference for single persons. Wear and tear, and thus repair costs, will usually be lower with single tenants than with families.

Paradoxical benefits for richer people

2. 'The aim of our housing policy is to favour the many poor and weak people, not the few rich'.

As wealth and income grew, people demanded more living space. Therefore, government housing experts believed that the demand for small apartments with one to two rooms would gradually decline. According to one of several false forecasts, a growing surplus of such dwellings would develop. In fact, the shortage had all the time been most pronounced in small apartments. The authorities, however, looked upon small apartments with aversion and contempt as something unworthy of the wealthy Swedish welfare state. They had, therefore, consistently directed construction towards large apartments. While the share of new dwellings with four rooms or more was 14 per cent in 1941 to 1945, this share had been raised to 37 per cent by 1966.

During recent times, a growing surplus of large expensive flats compels the authorities to retreat. Only high-income families can afford to rent them. At the same time there is a crying need for smaller apartments for families with low incomes. Judging from the practical results, one gets the impression that the policies pursued have had as a primary aim to favour the rich and few, not the poor and numerous.

Long waiting lists for the poor

3. 'In a free housing market the distribution of dwellings is determined by income. Through our "social housing policy" we have attempted to invalidate this rule. Not the size of the purse but the strength of the need shall decide the allocation of dwellings'.

Never before have people with low incomes found themselves in so weak and inferior positions as in the Swedish housing market. He who could only afford to rent a small dwelling could wait for years and years. The shortage was acute and the queues were long. Even families with children had to wait for years for dwellings of their own.

Large purses, of course, always meant advantages on the Swedish housing market, but never such enormous advantages as during the shortage years — the era of rent control. The rich man could solve his housing problem practically instantaneously. He could buy a house of his own. Or he could become part-owner of a cooperatively-built and owned property requiring a high investment in cash. Or he could rent a large, expensive, newly-built flat (of which there was a surplus). And, finally, he had the opportunity of acquiring an apartment in the black market (always possible, but very expensive). Not so the man with the low income.

VII. QUESTIONS AND ANSWERS ABOUT RENT CONTROL

> 'People complain that housing policy has become so complicated that they no longer understand it. But just imagine their complaints if they had understood it'.
> *The Economist*

1. *Is it really true that the abolition of rent control would introduce equilibrium in the housing market? Is the problem so simple?*

—Yes, certainly. According to general experience the price in a free market automatically creates equilibrium between supply and demand. Expenditures in Sweden on automobiles, TV sets, summer houses and foreign trips have increased at a much faster rate than expenditures on housing. Yet no signs of shortage have been noticed in these free markets.

That this situation can perplex even a Swedish Minister of Finance is evidenced by the following question:

> 'How is it possible that we can solve the economic problems when we wish to acquire a car or a TV set, but have so great difficulties with a need which is so morally well-founded as that of a dwelling?'[13]

2. *According to the critics, rent control creates both a shortage and a socially unacceptable distribution of dwellings. Unmarried persons with little need for dwellings of their own frequently displace married couples and families with more urgent requirements. Is not such a distribution even more characteristic of a free market, where wealthy persons with less pressing needs displace poor people with urgent requirements?*

—This objection can be met from the housing censuses undertaken in 1940 in the five cities of Nörrkoping, Västerås, Gävle, Kalmar and Kristianstad.[14] They show how the self-contained housing units available at that time (when the market was free) were distributed among the several groups of residents. Only 25 per cent of unmarried adults lived in their own dwellings, while the share of married people — with the most pressing need — was 97 per cent, and the previously married — with the next strongest need — 78 per cent. If a housing distribution authority had been responsible for the distribution, with 'social justice' as the criterion, one would have expected the figure to have been about the same. Therefore, the distribution mechanism of the free market is perhaps not so arbitrary.

3. *Would not the people in the old centrally-located residential areas be unjustly hit if rent control were abolished?*

[13]Gunnar Strang at the Conference of Riksbyggen (a construction co.) in June 1958

[14]*Sociala medd,* No. 3, 1951.

—No, they have been privileged for decades. Abolition of the privilege would mean a change but no injustice. The wasteful disposition of homes in these areas is the principal cause of the housing shortage. Better economy in their use would have given room to the homeless, too.

4. *Would not rent increases mean a lowering of standards by compelling more people to crowd into smaller and cheaper apartments?*

—The housing shortage has developed because the groups privileged by rent control have been able to increase their consumption of dwellings above that which would be allocated by the supply. A return to a free market would compel those privileged by rent control to give up some of their surplus or "luxury" space, and, as a result, dwellings would be made available for the homeless. A free housing market, therefore would mean a lower standard for those now privileged, but a very large improvement for those who now lack dwellings of their own. The housing shortage is essentially a problem of distribution.

5. *In a free housing market a natural reserve of empty flats always develops. Is not such an unused reserve an enormous waste?*

—On the contrary, it is the absence of a reserve of this kind that is wasteful because it prevents free mobility and free choice by the citizens. If we had had the same situation in our shops, their shelves would have been empty long since. The customers would have had to form a queue, fill in forms listing their requirements and then wait years for delivery.

6. *Would not abolition of rent control result in unjustifiable profits for the property owners?*

—The possibility of making profits is a driving force behind all private enterprise. Rising profits act as a signal to producers to increase the supply in the same way that falling profits (or losses) are a signal for a cessation of production. Normal development and expansion of private ownership and free enterprise is braked and prevented to the same degree as opportunities of making profits are curtailed.

Profits are in practice largely re-invested and function as a dynamic force for development and expansion. As a result of official attempts in Sweden to prevent private profits in housing, self-financing in this sector has gradually dwindled. The share of self-financing had in 1960 declined to 25 per cent and in 1970 to 10 per cent. It has been possible to provide the housing sector with necessary capital only by compulsory government measures. The sector has become parasitic; it can manage financially only by drawing capital from other sectors.

8

Decontrol

M.A. WALKER

*Chief Economist,
The Fraser Institute*

1975

THE AUTHOR

MICHAEL A. WALKER, PhD., is Chief Economist of The Fraser Institute. Born in Newfoundland in 1945, he received his B.A. (Summa) at St. Francis Xavier University and his PhD. in Economics at The University of Western Ontario, 1969. From 1969 to 1973, he worked in various research capacities at the Bank of Canada, Ottawa and when he left in 1973, was Research Officer in charge of the Special Studies and Monetary Policy group in the Department of Banking. Immediately prior to joining The Fraser Institute, Dr. Walker was Econometric Model Consultant to the Federal Department of Finance, Ottawa.

Decontrol

M.A. WALKER
Chief Economist,
The Fraser Institute

In some Canadian provinces rent control already exists in one form or another. Accordingly, having concluded that there is no case for rent control this monograph would not be complete without a consideration of the likely consequences of decontrol. Several suggestions of decontrol strategies are contained in the essays by Professor Paish and Professor Hayek. The essay by Professor Rydenfelt dealt with the unusual Swedish case of tenant pressure for decontrol. In this essay we consider some aspects of decontrol in theory and in practice. The practical evidence is derived from the U.S. experience with decontrol because it is the case where detailed information is available.

Is a decontrol 'strategy' necessary?

The presumption that a decontrol strategy is necessary embodies some of the same concerns that led to control in the first place. Basically, these boil down to a fear that the return to a free market will impose 'undue' hardship. Typically, the hardship alluded to is that low income groups will be forced to pay an unrealistic portion of their income for rental accommodation. (The particular plight of low-income homeowners caught between the jaws of a relatively fixed income and rising property taxes is seemingly not a matter for concern in any of the debates about control).

It is clear, however, that if hardship for low-income groups does occur, it is a result of an inadequate income-supplementation scheme and should be treated as such. If the "hardship" referred to is the fact that all consumers will, upon decontrol, have to pay a market rent for accommodation, it is very difficult to be sympathetic to this view.[1] The costs of adjustment back to a market rent will fall on roughly the same group of people who enjoyed the "benefits" that accrued from control. (Except to the extent that people lower the quantity or quality of housing services that they buy as a result of the return to a market price).

Apart from the hollow ring of the general hardship rationale, the case for some sort of gradual decontrol has a bothersome internal inconsistency. The removal of rent control is a tacit recognition that its disincentive effects produce undesirable results in the supply of rental accommodation, the burden of which is ultimately borne by *tenants.* In other words, rent control is a tax that landlords attempt to avoid by not offering additional rental accommodation. They simply invest their capital elsewhere. Once this recognition has been made it seems at least 'passing curious' to adopt the position that a gradual removal is called for.

A related point is the fact that the imposition of control has the effect of increasing the riskiness of investment in rental housing. (Even if it is dropped, will it be tried again?) Accordingly, control and the fear of control have the effect of increasing the rate of return that landlords require from investment in housing. The shift away from controls ought, therefore, to be accomplished with a view to restoring investors' confidence in the intentions of the government. A prolonged 'period of adjustment' does not promise to have this effect.

The "political realities"

If there is any rationale for rent control, it is probably that it is a very effective device for attracting the votes of tenants — at least in the short run. Given that fact, the most vociferous defenders of a gradual decontrol system are likely to be the politicians responsible for the control or analysts who take pride in the political pragmatism of their policy advice: "A successful argument for decontrol is the

[1] Indeed it could be argued that, since the inducement to supply housing has been depressed by the controls, a subsidy be given to landlords to induce them back into the construction of rental housing. *The cost of this subsidy ought to be borne by those who benefitted from the controls,* other than low-income groups.

one that the politicians accept — any proposal earnestly designed to achieve decontrol must encompass these realities!"

This sort of approach makes one begin to realize the devastating accuracy of Gunnar Myrdal's observation that:

> . . . "Rent control in certain western countries constituted, maybe, the worst example of poor planning by governments lacking in *courage and vision*".[2]

The fact is that the economic realities are very different from those perceived by people concerned about the political realities. The overriding fear is that return to a market situation will bring in its wake very rapid rises in rents — a politically devastating occurrence. It is this 'bogeyman' waiting in the wings that causes all the concern for a 'politically acceptable' decontrol strategy.

Debunking the 'bogeyman'

The only experience with decontrol that has been accurately recorded, of which we are aware, was that undertaken in the United States in the last months of 1949. The U.S. Department of Labor conducted surveys in cities that were decontrolled to determine rents before and after decontrol. The results of this survey are contained in Exhibit 1.

At the time decontrol came, in the last months of 1949, rent control had been in effect for eight years. During that period a general wage and price freeze was in effect. The general wage and price controls — except for rent — were dropped in 1946 under the pressure of events. (There were strikes in key industries because companies subject to price control could not yield to even the reasonable demands of unions; shortages of various foods such as beef, butter and oranges developed and there was a general proliferation of supply crises and their bedfellows — black markets). From 1946 to the end of 1949, the general price level in the U.S. rose by 32.4 percent — a very large increase by the then existing historical standards.[3]

[2]Quoted in, "The Rise and Fall of Swedish Rent Control", this volume.

[3]U.S. Department of Labor, Bureau of Labor Statistics, Monthly Labor Review, various years.

Against this backdrop of general inflation, rents in aggregate rose by only 14.5 percent over the 1946-1949 period[4] and in the year of widespread decontrol, rents rose by only 3.5 percent. In fact, it was not until 1954 that rents caught up with the level of other prices.

Exhibit 1 — Increases in Rents Free to Rise after Termination of Federal Rent Control in Cities

ALL RENT RANGES

(EXCLUDES UNITS HAVING CONTINUOUS LEASES AND UNITS INDIVIDUALLY DECONTROLLED BEFORE AREA-WIDE DECONTROL)

City	Percent of All units Having Increases	Their Average Percentage Increase	Average Percentage Increase In General Rent Level*	Survey	Date of Decontrol
Houston, Texas	31	41.3	10.7	8/15/49-11/15/49	10/19
Beverly Hills, Calif.	74	41.0	26.7	10/15/49-3/1/50	12/7
Dallas, Texas	67	35.4	20.5	4/15/49-11/15/49	6/23
Topeka, Kansas	40	30.3	10.5	7/15/49-11/15/49	9/14
Eugene, Oregon	38	30.3	9.4	6/15/49-2/15/50	8/18
Knoxville, Tennessee	61	26.8	15.8	5/15/49-11/15/49	6/14
Jacksonville, Fla.	56	26.2	12.3	6/15/49-11/15/49	8/5
Oklahoma City, Okla.[1]	17	26.2	2.9	9/15/49-1/15/50	11/23
Omaha, Nebraska	62	21.9	14.2	9/15/49-1/15/50	11/2
Milwaukee, Wisc.[2]	60	20.2	12.2	5/15/49-2/15/50	8/5
Spokane, Washington	46	18.6	8.2	5/15/49-11/15/49	7/25
Witchita, Kansas	35	18.2	6.4	10/15/49-3/1/50	12/29
Salt Lake City, Utah	46	16.2	7.1	6/15/49-11/15/49	8/5
Madison, Wisc.	51	12.3	5.9	6/15/49-2/15/50	8/5

[1]General Rent Increase of 20 Percent granted prior to decontrol; [2]Includes all units — data on rents free to rise not available; *(Includes rents which did not increase).

Source: "Hearings before the Committee on Banking and Currency, United States Senate", 1950, *Extension of Rent Control*, p. 462. Reprinted in "The Post War Rent Control Controversy", by Willys R. Knight, Director, Bureau of Business and Economic Research, Georgia State College, Research Paper Number 23, September 1962.

The data in Exhibit 1 indicate that only in three cases did the rent increase after decontrol exceed 15 per cent. (Dallas, Beverley Hills and Knoxville). The average percentage increase in rents amounted to only 11.6 per cent. Thus, it can hardly be said that decontrol produced skyrocketing rents or housing market chaos or any of the other consequences that are often feared.

[4]Some increases had been allowed by the "Housing Expediter" who was responsible for the administration of rent control.

Altruistic landlords?

Why didn't rents rise much more quickly? Surely, given the general rate of inflation and the rapid rise in costs, landlords would have wanted much larger increases? The answer is that what landlords want to charge does not determine market rents — even in a so-called shortage situation. The market level of rents is determined both by what landlords want to charge and by what tenants are willing to pay. If rents rise too sharply, relative to other prices and relative to incomes, many tenants — especially singles and married couples without children — move to smaller accommodation or "double-up" and landlords are left with vacant suites. The competition between different landlords trying to keep all of their suites occupied — given consumer resistance — is the ultimate check on the increase in rents.

Bogeymen die hard

It is always interesting to examine the outcome of events about which there has been much speculation. In the case of rent control in the U.S. the retrospective view is not only interesting but very informative. The Federal Government's Housing Expediter, Mr. Tighe Woods, was a staunch supporter of continued control over rents, and until the municipalities and cities were given responsibility for decontrol, very few communities (largely small centres of population) were, in fact, freed from controls by Woods.

Once control was made a local option, many communities immediately decontrolled and "the situation was accepted quietly and with only a moderate degree of rental increase".[5] The interesting aspect of these moves to decontrol is the fact that in almost every instance they were taken "in spite of findings and warnings from the Housing Expediter that a continuation of controls were (sic) essential".[6]

[5]The Post War Rent Control Controversy, Research Report 23, W.R. Knight, Director, Bureau of Business and Economic Research, Georgia State College, Sept. 1962. Page 22.

[6]Ibid, Page 23.

Bogeyman's last stand

The most interesting example, perhaps, is that of Los Angeles, which the Housing Expediter adopted as a *cause célèbre*. In July, 1950, the City Council of Los Angeles adopted a resolution that said in effect that rent control was no longer required because there was no housing shortage. The Housing Expediter disagreed and maintained that the facts indicated a continuing critical housing shortage and, therefore, the council could not legally decontrol the city.

The city council had, prior to its decision, conducted a comprehensive survey of housing conditions in Los Angeles (April, 1950). That survey, which gathered many pertinent details including rents asked, whether children were accepted, etc., indicated that nearly three per cent of the city's housing units were vacant. The council concluded that no shortage existed. The Housing Expediter viewed this same information as indicating that an acute housing shortage still existed, largely on the basis of the fact that the vacancy rate was below 5 per cent.

In the event, Mr. Woods went to the courts and secured an injunction to halt decontrol. The result was that decontrol was postponed for six months. In the end, the Los Angeles City Council's view prevailed and on December 20, 1950, controls were abandoned.

> "No riots or mass evictions developed. Most observers agreed that the rent increases which resulted were moderate. 'For Rent' columns appeared again in the newspapers, and the shortage was deemed to be over. *In the aldermanic elections held the following spring* (several months after decontrol), *rent control was not an issue. Nine of the ten aldermen who had voted for* decontrol were re-elected . . ."[7]

Los Angeles proved to be the bellwether for the rest of the country, and from the time that Los Angeles was decontrolled, many cities took action to decontrol. The decontrol process was complete in the U.S. before the Korean War ended, except in New York City, where it lingers still.

[7]Ibid. Page 24.

Conclusions about decontrol

The evidence from post war decontrol in the U.S. indicates that, even in an inflationary period, removal of rent control does not lead to excessive increases in rents. This is probably because the demand for rental housing services is sufficiently elastic to prevent landlords from 'making up' the shortfall (caused by control) in a short period of time. Furthermore, as the particular case of Los Angeles clearly demonstrates, the concern of elected officials that decontrol means disaster is not a well-founded one. Accordingly, the principal concern of the architects of a decontrol "strategy" ought to be to repair the "damage" that has been done to the supply of rental housing — i.e., investor confidence, and not the bogeyman of "political realities".

PART III

What Is The Solution?

An Income Supplement Program

M.A. WALKER

Introduction and summary

Before presenting a solution to what we have identified as the problem it is perhaps useful to recapitulate the findings thus far.

In Part I we set out to determine what the nature of "the housing problem" is and we found, as others have found, that the problem is basically an income problem. The current tendency for rents to rise was identified as an inevitable consequence of rising costs and market adjustment to changes in Federal Tax laws. This rise in rents is not, in itself, a "problem" since it is essential if the construction of rental accommodation is to be undertaken. The current lack of rental housing construction is a direct consequence of the fact that rents are too low and once rents have adjusted to an appropriate level rental housing construction will resume. As the market adjusts, however, the cost of basic shelter may rise and this may inflict hardship on low income groups whose incomes do not keep pace with the increase in rents. This is the real "problem".

In Part II we provided essays by distinguished academics on the effects of rent control in several different countries in a variety of historical time periods. The unanimous conclusion of these authors is that rent control does not solve either the income problem of low-income groups or the "problem" of lack of rental housing construction. In fact, the conclusion is that rent control makes matters considerably worse and should, therefore, be avoided. It was observed, furthermore, that this low opinion of rent control is shared by all economists regardless of their ideological bent.

An examination of the available evidence on the effects of decontrol produced the conclusion that the effects of decontrol are likely to be much less severe than is often supposed, owing largely to consumer resistance. There appears to be no real reason for a gradual decontrol strategy.

The lesson of the essays for legislators is, if you have the best interest of tenants in mind don't control rents and if you already have control then *decontrol* as quickly as possible. Since there is, however, a possibility that this will cause undue hardship for low income groups, some sort of social assistance program related to the cost of basic shelter could be implemented, provided the total of all government expenditures are not either: A. at an inflationary level or B. thereby caused to be inflationary. The consequence of these two restrictions for Canada in 1975 is probably that a housing supplementation program must be integrated into current government expenditures and replace rather than extend existing programs.

Assuming that such a program can be accommodated within the existing structure of expenditures, the purpose of this essay is to present a method for achieving an income supplement that would relieve the hardship of low-income groups, or, at least remove the hardship that arises to the extent that the cost of basic accommodation is high relative to their incomes and may, although that is unlikely, represent a higher proportion of their incomes as time passes. There are two basic forms that a housing subsidy can take, each of which reflects a different social objective.

The objective of increasing choice

One possible objective of an income supplement is to provide the recipients with a wider range of discretion in the disposal of their incomes. In the case of housing, the supplement is normally motivated by the observation that some people are spending a large proportion of their income on housing. From this observation it is inferred that people so affected must be suffering hardship because, having paid "for a roof over their heads", they have very little left for the necessities of life and none for life's pleasures.

If lack of an effective discretionary income is the problem, then the subsidy should take the form of an income supplement or an unrestricted cash grant, as Professor Olsen calls it in his essay.

Housing conditions objective

An objective of a different sort is that of ensuring that everybody in the community actually lives (as opposed to, can afford to live) in housing of not less than some minimum standard. In this case the objective is not to increase the discretionary income of the poor, but to directly raise their standard of housing. Presumably, this objective embodies the judgment that people should live in good housing, *whether they want to or not,* because the existence of substandard housing creates other social problems.

If the objective is to coerce people to raise their standard of housing, then the subsidy must be tied directly to housing, either in the form of a housing "chit" or in the form of a public housing scheme.

Our preference

The subsidy developed here is of the income supplement variety. It is preferred over the direct housing subsidy because the direct subsidy has the effect of forcing the recipients to conform to the community's notion of a minimum standard of housing. Since one of the objectives of government policy ought to be the maximization of individual choice, it is difficult to accept a social assistance scheme that is based on the principle of coercion. For the same reason, the subsidy should be extended to all Canadians whether they choose to own or rent accommodation.

Another reason for preferring an income supplement is that it leaves the business of the provision of housing to the private sector. The private sector has provided Canadians with a standard of housing that is among the highest in the world. There seems little reason to interfere directly with this mechanism which, as we saw in the first essay of Part I, seems to work remarkably well, in spite of the buffeting it receives from government policies.

The shelter cost-to-income ratio

In a 1972 study of low-income housing, Michael Dennis and Susan Fish[1] suggested two different schemes for calculating the amount of an income supplement to offset the cost of housing. Both of these schemes were based on the notion that the objective is to lower the fraction of income that poor people *must spend* to provide themselves with housing. The essential element in their formulae is a target shelter cost-to-income ratio of 20 per cent. That is, the objective of their formulae is to provide an income supplement which would ensure that no Canadians *actually spend* more than 20 per cent of their income on housing. (There is an important difference between what people *must spend* and what they *actually do spend.* More is said below about this difference and the effect it has on a subsidy program.)

Their two proposals are:

1. Provide a supplement to each member of an income group equal to the difference between (a) the fraction of income that the group, on average, actually spent on shelter, and (b) 20 per cent; multiplied by the average income of the group. This would bring the average shelter cost-to-income ratio of the group down to 20 per cent.

Using numbers roughly the same as the figures in Exhibit 7, we can calculate what that housing subsidy would have been in 1972 for the lowest income group.

Average Shelter Cost-to-Income Ratio	= .3 = 30%
Assume average income of people in the less than $4,000 per year income group was $3,000.	
Target Shelter Cost-to-Income Ratio	= .2 = 20%
Difference between Actual and Target Shelter Cost-to-Income Ratio	.3 - .2 = .1
Income Supplement	= .1 x $3,000 = $300

[1]Programs in Search of a Policy — *Low Income Housing in Canada,* Hakkert, Toronto, 1972, Pages 354-360.

2. Their second proposal is similar to the first, except that instead of using the average shelter cost-to-income ratio for the group, the calculation employs the actual shelter cost-to-income ratio for the individual recipient.

Recipient's shelter cost-to-income ratio	35%
Recipient's Income	$2,500
Target Shelter Cost-to-Income Ratio	.2 = 20%
Difference between Actual and Target	= .35 - .2 = .15
Income Supplement	= .15 x $2,500 = $375.

Difficulties with the Dennis and Fish Formulae

One obvious problem with these formulae is that they do not relate the amount of the income supplement to the actual cost of basic accommodation, a defect which, in our opinion, makes them totally unacceptable. On the other hand, they do provide an incentive for people to devote an increased fraction of their income to housing, because the amount of the subsidy is tied to shelter expenditures. For example, an individual, in the case of the second formula, would be encouraged by the form of the supplement program to either spend, or make it seem as if he were spending, a very high proportion of his income on shelter. The formula would ensure that he received an income supplement to offset this increase in housing expenditures. The experience with other social assistance plans (like unemployment benefits) indicates that there is no end to the ingenuity that people apply in abusing a system if it is not absolutely free of loopholes. This should be enough to warn-off legislators from Formula 2.

Formula 1 has the distinct drawback that if housing expenditures respond to the level of income (and the evidence suggests that they do)[2], then the subsidy scheme could produce a preposterous outcome in very short notice.

[2]See L.B. Smith, Op. Cit., Page 63; also, Dennis and Fish, Op. Cit., Page 357.

For example, suppose that the formula is applied as above and that the subsidy recipients spend about half of the income supplement that they receive to upgrade their housing conditions.

The sequence of income supplements in the first and following years would be as follows:

Year 1	Housing expenditures	$ 900
	Average Income	$3,000
	Income Supplement	$ 300
Year 2	Housing expenditures	$900 Plus half of supplement, $150 = $1,050
	Average Income	= $3,300
	Shelter-to-Income Ratio in second year	$= \frac{\$1,050}{3,300} = .318 = 31.8\%$
	Target Ratio	= .2 = 20%
	Income Supplement in Year Two	= (.318 - .2) x 3,300 = $389.40
Year 3	Housing expenditures $1,050	
		Plus half of new income supplement $194.70 = $1,244.70
	Income Supplement in Year 3	= $566.70
Year 4	Housing expenditures	$1,528.05
	Income Supplement in Year 4	= $814.63

If we had assumed that less than half of the income supplement is used by the low-income groups to upgrade their housing standard, then the result would be somewhat different. As long as some of the income supplement is spent in this way, however, the income supplement under this formula would increase from year to year simply because the income group in question was spending some of the subsidy on housing. If the percentage of the subsidy that the group spends on housing is less than the overall ratio of their housing expenditures to their income (which is unlikely), then the increase in the subsidy from year to year would get smaller and smaller until it became negligible.

Protection from what?

In other words, these formulae do not protect people from the hardship caused by what they *must* spend on shelter but from the seeming hardship that occurs because of what they *do* spend. The amount they *do* spend could, of course, be greater or less than the amount that they *must* spend to acquire basic accommodation, since they may or may not inhabit accommodation that is regarded as basic.

Our conclusions on the Dennis and Fish formulae is that they have several built-in limitations, and accordingly, should be avoided. The formula suggested in the following section does not have deficiencies of the sort outlined above (although it may have some of which we are not aware) and is our suggested scheme.

A Housing Income Supplement

The characteristics of the proposed income supplementation formula are as follows:

1. The amount of the income supplement is tied directly to the cost of basic accommodation for each type of recipient and not, as the Dennis and Fish supplements are, to the actual shelter expenditures of recipients.

2. The formula provides a supplement that is determined by the cost of basic shelter in the area where the recipient lives, and would provide in itself no incentive to the recipient to move from one region to another (which would obviously be the effect of a supplement program that did not reflect regional differences in the cost of housing).

3. The formula provides a flexibility in the target shelter cost-to-income ratio that is reflected in the income supplement itself.

4. There is an automatic change in the income supplement to reflect changing circumstances, but since the supplement is tied to the cost of basic accommodation, it will tend to rise much more slowly than an expenditure-based subsidy of the Dennis and Fish variety.

The details

Essentially, the formula is designed to calculate a housing allowance that ensures that Canadians do not have to spend more than X per cent of their income to provide themselves with basic shelter. The basic element of the formula is the dollar cost of basic shelter (room, light and heat) for an individual, a family of two, family of three, etc., depending on the size of the recipient household. The formula implements the judgment that the cost of *basic* accommodation as a percentage of the recipients income ought not to exceed X per cent. The provision is that the income of a particular recipient has to equal at least the minimum cost of basic accommodation for that recipient (not what the recipient actually spends) divided by the target income proportion.[3] The income supplement would be calculated as the difference between the target income (a dollar amount, of which basic accommodation cost is exactly X percent) and the actual income of the recipient:

$$\text{Supplement} = \left(\frac{\text{Cost of Basic Accommodation}}{\text{Target Shelter Cost-to-income ratio}}\right) \text{ minus } \left(\begin{array}{c}\text{Actual Income}\\ \text{of Recipient}\end{array}\right)$$

Implementation

The cost of basic accommodation should be calculated by the Department of Housing in each province as an average of the actual cost of providing weatherproof shelter, heat and light, such that each person in a family group has access to a minimum of 1.6 rooms of living space. (The average for Canadians is 1.6)

[3]Let \$C be the cost of basic accommodation and Y be the target income based on the target shelter cost ratio. X is the target shelter cost-to-income ratio and \$S is the income supplement. \$I is the person's actual income.

The formula says $\frac{\$C}{Y}$ should be equal to X

So, $\frac{\$C}{Y} = X$, or $Y = \frac{\$C}{X}$

If Y is greater than the recipients actual income then a subsidy is given equal to the difference between the target income and the actual income $\$S = Y - \$I$.

An example: Suppose the minimum cost of *basic* shelter is \$100 per month for a two member family. Suppose that the provincial government has selected 25 per cent as the target shelter cost-to-income ratio. The target monthly income for a two member family is thus 100./.25 = \$400 per month. If a particular two member family's income was \$350 per month, then the subsidy would be \$400 - \$350 = \$50 per month.

The most difficult decision that must be made is the selection of an appropriate shelter cost-to-income ratio. The selection process should recognize the fact that too large a subsidy would, like all social assistance programs, encourage people to attempt to qualify by lowering their incomes or by falsifying their income declarations. On the other hand, the program should, at the outset, reduce the hardship of those people at the very bottom of the income scale.

According to the most recent data available (Exhibit 7), Canadians, on average, spend 16.1 per cent of their income on shelter. The poorest income group, on the other hand, spends 30.7 per cent on shelter. The percentage of all Canadians in the low income group is falling steadily (in the interval 1969-1971 it fell from 16.9 per cent to 13.3 per cent of all Canadians) and accordingly, the actual number of people who are paying as high as 30.7 per cent of their income on shelter has been falling year by year. A reasonable objective of a housing subsidy scheme would be to accelerate this process.

It is in that spirit that the following method is outlined. The target shelter cost-to-income ratio should be selected in each year so as to eradicate, say, 25 per cent of the difference between the *basic shelter cost-to-income ratio*[4] of the lowest income group and the average for all Canadians. So, for example, in 1975 the target shelter cost-to-income ratio should be 27.1 per cent (using the data in Exhibit 7 and assuming that the shelter expenditure of the lowest income groups represented basic shelter expenditures). In the following years, 25 per cent of the remaining gap would be eliminated until ultimately the gap became negligible.

Self-liquidating

In spite of the fact that this scheme would eradicate the gap, it would probably (on the basis of the historical evidence) involve progressively smaller total subsidy costs — thus, the program would be self-liquidating. There are two reasons for this. First of all, the amount of the subsidy for any individual is tied to the cost of basic accommodation because the target income used to calculate the supplement is determined

[4]which, it should be noted, is different than the shelter-to-income ratio which may include more or less than *basic* shelter costs.

largely by the cost of basic accommodation. Historically, the cost of basic accommodation (and hence "target income") has fallen relative to incomes and will probably continue to fall in relative terms. Hence, as time passes, the actual amount of the subsidy, which is the difference between target and actual income, for each eligible individual will fall. Secondly, as incomes grow there will be fewer people in the lower income groups and, hence, the subsidy will apply to fewer people.

An income supplement for landlords?

Throughout our discussion to this point we have ignored the arguments raised by opponents of shelter allowances. In this section we shall deal with their reservations. The essence of the argument is that the allowance will be lost in the form of higher rents and, the opponents of shelter allowances say, the allowance ends up as an increase in landlords' incomes. Thus, the allowance does not result in an improved situation for low-income tenants.

Like many of the propositions advanced by protagonists in the housing debate, there appears to be little, if any, evidence to support this contention. What evidence there is suggests that less than one dollar in seven of a shelter allowance is likely to accrue to the landlord in the form of higher rents[5] This is partly due to the fact that not all of the shelter allowance would be spent on shelter and partly due to the fact that rents rise, proportionately, less than housing demand. The latter fact is reflected in rent and income statistics, which show that in spite of the fact that incomes have risen by 220 per cent in the past 14 years, rents, for a given standard of housing, have risen by only 30 per cent. On the basis of this historical relationship one would expect, on average, about one dollar in seven of an income supplement to be "lost" in the form of higher rents. This confirms the impression gained from the evidence cited by Dennis and Fish. (Footnote 5).

It is undoubtedly true, however, that some recipients of a shelter allowance would be victimized by unscrupulous landlords. Aged tenants or those who are for other reasons

[5]Dennis and Fish, *Op. Cit.*, Pages 357-358.

not mobile would be unable to avoid the demands of a landlord who wanted to take advantage of the fact that this sort of tenant is not protected by the normal interplay of competitive forces. Although this sort of landlord is probably rare, it would be unrealistic to assume that they do not exist.

It is also probably true that some ineligible tenants would fraudulently obtain an income supplement. However, if one were to access every social assistance scheme and reject those that had abuses or leakages associated with them, it is hard to imagine one that would be retained. Thus, although an income supplementation scheme would be imperfect, this is not a reflection on the shelter supplement scheme, but an inherent characteristic of all social assistance programs.

An obvious shortcoming?

Some readers will, doubtless, have come to the conclusion that the income supplementation formula suggested here has a very obvious defect. Since the formula is critically dependent on the cost of *basic* shelter and since everybody knows that the notion of *basic* shelter is very difficult to define, isn't the proposed formula unworkable?

It is certainly true that what constitutes *basic* shelter is a fundamental difficulty, but avoiding the issue, as formulae that do not include the cost of basic shelter effectively do, does not make the issue disappear. In fact, the determination of what constitutes "hardship" and the definition of "basic shelter" are the crucial issues in the matter of housing assistance programs. The failure to deal with these issues directly constitutes a failure to deal with the problem.

Behind the design of every social assistance program lurks a fundamental danger — one which is verbalized less today than it should be. This danger can be summarized in three questions:

1. At what point does the sum of all government social assistance programs produce structural inflation?
2. At what point does a social assistance program destroy the incentive for people to improve their own economic situation?

3. At what point does assumption of the responsibility for the solution of economic problems of choice by the state lead to a total loss of the ability to make individual choices of any kind?

Although housing policy is only one element of social policy, the framers of housing legislation cannot avoid these fundamental questions.